Crashes & Prangs

Aircraft that have Suffered Mishap through Fair Means or Foul

by

Arthur W. J. G. Ord-Hume

D1331048

One characteristic of the very earliest aircraft is that due to their method of construction when they were damaged (which was rather frequently) repairs were usually simple to undertake. Even when quite severe accidents dramatically altered the shape of an aeroplane, restitution to flyable condition was usually possible quite quickly. Here is a Caudron biplane of a type first seen at the Paris Salon on December 16th 1911. It was offered for sale at £320 new and 'guaranteed to fly at 55 miles an hour'. At Hendon, the well-known flyer W H Ewen took delivery of one on Saturday April 20th 1912. William H Ewen was born in Glasgow and resided in Lanark. An early flying enthusiast, he learned to fly at Hendon on a Blériot Monoplane, took his Certificate Number 63 on February 14th 1911, and went straight back to Scotland to open a flying school on Lanark Racecourse which he leased. It did not enjoy much following and the local council feared that Ewen's under-use would not be good for business. But Ewen could not pluck business out of thin air and so he packed up. The following year he was back at Hendon where he set up a successful flying school and also had (for a short while) the rights to distribute the Caudron in Britain. At the Whitsun race meeting of 1912 he was cornering around a pylon too steeply and too low when he was hit by a gust of wind that winged him into the ground. The pilot escaped with painful cuts and bruises and the aeroplane was taken away to be rebuilt. Curiously Ewen faded from the scene in 1914 and his fate cannot now be readily traced.

First Published in the United Kingdom, 2010
Stenlake Publishing Limited
54-58 Mill Square, Catrine, KA5 6RD
www.stenlake.co.uk

ISBN 9781840334906

In the earliest years of British aviation, there were very many accidents, not all of them fatal. Those that people recall are the ones that marked a turning point in the development of the aeroplane. The mishap that befell Hon C S Rolls (of Rolls-Royce renown) was one and that of 'Colonel' Cody another. A third was that of 27-year-old Graham Gilmour (born 1885) for whom there was immense affection and respect from an aviation-minded population that flocked to Hendon or Brooklands every week to watch the flying. He was described by chronicler Dallas Brett as 'one of the ten best British pilots'. On February 17th 1912, Gilmour's luck ran out when his Antoinette-engined Martin-Handasyde monoplane left Brooklands on a short local flight. In turbulent air over the Old Deer Park at Richmond something went wrong and his fragile machine fell to earth from a height of about 400 feet. He was killed instantly. Nobody ever found out quite what happened although reports that a wing fell off in the air were not totally supported by examination of the wreckage. It was later determined that somehow the left wing broke in rough air, a new pair of wings having been fitted only the previous day. Accident investigation was at that time even more elemental than flying itself.

Introduction

Let's get one thing straight right from the start. I don't think there's anything in any way funny, amusing or entertaining about an aircraft accident. I have been involved in a few flying mishaps in my time and none that I recall generated the slightest sense of anything other than pain (in various quantities), anguish for my broken chariot of the Heavens, and embarrassment for being too closely involved when it happened. There wasn't any feeling of achievement (save that of survival), let alone joviality – and precious little enjoyment.

These days popular computer websites and TV programmes revealing people making fools of themselves show flying accidents as a source of certain amusement for a sad minority amongst the chattering classes who find mirth in almost any sort of adversity. No, be certain that my interest in aircraft is in keeping them in one piece, airworthy and, above all, preserving the good people that fly in them. Bending an aeroplane is, to my way of thinking, a sin.

That isn't to blot out the fact that since the very earliest times there has always been two ways of getting back to earth at the end of a flight – the conventional, soft way or, as an alternative, the spectacular way usually accompanied by the splintering of wood, tearing of metal and ripping of doped fabric. The macho pilot of old was reputed to allege that any landing you could walk away from was a good landing. Personally that sounds like the prattle of the man who flies somebody else's aeroplane – a legacy, perhaps, of the early days at Hendon and the dark days of RFC training when you were just as likely to be killed learning to fly as by getting involved with an adversary's gun-sight.

There remains in most of us an unusual interest in accidents of every kind. I have avoided using the word 'unhealthy' because if it were then it would be verging on the epidemic. Early movie-makers revelled in staging head-on train crashes preserved on celluloid while today's Hollywood 'blockbusters' are nothing without spectacular car crashes, ships detonating devastatingly, skyscrapers ablaze and people being rendered into their component parts by explosion.

Flying mishaps appeal to the primordial or intuitive part of our mentality that relishes the spectacular, curiously exploits danger and associates risks and risk-taking with adventure. But that's something I at least cannot explain. What I do know is that it's often possible to learn something from an accident by the way it has unfolded even if it is only the miserably elemental fact of the way something breaks when overloaded. All aircraft accidents are horrible and pictures of them preserve for others that moment of abject terror when somebody faces a peril that is as unfathomable as it is fearsome. At the very least it sees the almost instantaneous conversion of somebody's pride and joy aeroplane – the product of dedicated and dexterous people who have devoted many hours (and much money) to its construction – from superlative denizen of the skies to a tangle of terrible scrap. Rest assured, there's no amusement there.

People get hurt in accidents and that again is no cause for sensationalism. And when a life is spent as the result of a flying accident that is a whole different story. Heaven (and, possibly, the other place) is populated with one-time friends who have paid the final price for being adventurous and unlucky, careless and unwise.

I did say that no accident is a cause for merriment. A prang isn't 'funny' as such. But I have to admit to a wry smile when, only a short while ago, an elderly German couple were flying their light aircraft over their home skies when, with vision restricted by a low evening sun, they had the misfortune to 'land' on some hitherto unseen high-tension cables. The wheels caught on the wires, the aeroplane stopped and was left hanging largely upside down, unharmed but embarrassingly obvious for all around to see. Pilot and his passenger then spent some hours upside down in the cabin gently bouncing up and down in silence while rescuers thought of a way to get them down safely. A high-lift platform and some brave men tempted fate to open the cabin door and ease out the unharmed pair. And the next day an even higher crane rescued their aeroplane, causing far more damage sorting out that last seventy feet or so to the ground than the actual mishap itself. That sort of adventure is all too easy to happen and there are too many pictures I have of burned-up aircraft hanging in electricity cables in America and Canada.

Some years back, when I was associated with Britten-Norman Ltd on the Isle of Wight, we had a very experienced ferry pilot take off to ferry one of our Islander aircraft 'over the top' to Canada. His passage across the frozen wastes of Greenland was so far north as to make compass bearings rather uncertain. An unexpected and, more important, undetected strong wind had also pushed him far, far off course. Unaware of all this and cruising along merrily at what looked like about 11,500 feet in a total visibility 'white-out', he had the curious experience of suddenly stopping! The engines still ran but the aircraft had simply come to a halt. Puzzled – and still apparently at 11,500 feet – he switched off the engines, opened the door and stepped out into thick snow. He was, of course, on top of a mountain! Dead lucky to get away with it so far, he now faced his greatest challenge for he wasn't dressed for arctic mountaineering and suffered enormous privations struggling his way to civilisation and eventual survival. That accident was, for some of us, slightly amusing and six months later a team went out and salvaged the undamaged aircraft.

My old friend Harold Best-Devereux took off from Elstree on a post-C of A test flight in a sleek newly-refinished Miles cabin monoplane but, just clear of the end of the runway, he experienced engine failure. Nose down he made for a field only to find that he was under a pair of converging high-tension National Grid power lines. Touch-down was in extremely tall grass a few yards from where the lines met at one stout pylon. Brand new fabric and an expensive paint scheme had to be ripped away to take the wings off and bring the undamaged pilot and aircraft back to the workshops.

Another time I happened to be beside the clubhouse phone when it rang. 'I've broken my propeller and I'm down in a large playing field.' It was a friend of mine who flew for the famous Aerofilms company that was based at Elstree. Glad of the opportunity to fly and knowing just where he was, I told him I was on my way with a spare 'screw and to wait for my arrival. I grabbed some tools, put the replacement propeller diagonally across the Auster cabin and set off for the wilds of Leicestershire. Soon I spotted the crippled G-AGXH (that's newspaper speak: *all* downed aircraft are 'crippled') next to goal-posts in a large field. Inevitably its presence had attracted a sizeable crowd of spectators but happily they parted as I landed. Whatever the Aerofilms machine had hit (I suspect it was a duck-sized bird), half of one blade was missing and he'd been lucky to get down safely. As we began removing the shattered remains, the Law arrived, naturally on an aged bike. He was a ruddy-faced clummock of a policeman and I guessed there was going to be a problem the moment the well-thumbed notebook appeared and the pencil end was licked.

He didn't like planes. Dangerous things they were, he said. And we had crash-landed (his words, not mine) in his 'patch'. Had we permission to make use of the playing field and did we know this, that and the other. All the while we kept working as I explained something of the emergency, the mercy flight (more newspaper speak!) and the reason for two identical Austers on this piece of isolated grassland. He then did something unexpected – he announced he was going to telephone his 'super' and we were to await his return: remember this was in the peaceful days before mobile phones. As he set off to a far-off red box in a middle-distance lane, we completed the job and I quickly tracked the replacement prop.

All being spot-on and tickety-boo, we considered our position and came to the conclusion that it would be a good idea for us not to be around when PC Clummock returned. He propped me, I propped him – and we roared off between the goal-posts into the welcoming blue and back to Elstree. Curiously we never heard any more about this incident.

The Ultra Light Aircraft Association held its summer camp at Redhill one year, sharing facilities and aircraft with the nubile ladies of the Women's Junior Air Corps. The sight of these young girls running around in terribly short shorts and the briefest of thin cotton tops made for a rather high-octane atmosphere. And so when their Piper Cub overshot on approach and came down (thankfully safely) in a nearby sewage farm's grounds, every young man worth his salt fancied his chances at dashing in and carrying out the semi-naked young lady who timorously called for help from within the undamaged Cub. But they each stopped dead in their tracks at the boundary fence. Like all sewage farms, this one was nurturing acres of spectacularly large and vicious-looking stinging nettles! That day rescue was not by an eager young man with fast-beating heart and a hunched posture. Gallant Sir Gallahad turned out to be a stoutly-clad aerodrome-mower tractor-driver in tough dungarees who unhesitatingly went in and rescued a very shaken but grateful young lady.

So why a picture book of what in the Royal Air Force we used to term as 'prangs'? Well, there's a certain excitement in that moment of horror and some of the mishaps over the years have been interesting and spectacular. If you will pardon a dreadful pun, my collection of prang pictures started rather by accident when I took some pictures of one of my own mishaps. I then began collecting others until I had a huge box full. I quickly add that they were not *all* of my own prangs.

How does this book work? Well, I have attempted to avoid those accidents that have left people dead and maimed although this association cannot be avoided in all instances. You will find no gory or gruesome images in here for what I have done is tried to choose pictures of the unusual. The preference is thus for the ones that have made an impression on me. Some are long-forgotten while others are still in the memory of some of my readers. And some 'prangs' aren't really accidents at all, merely amusing instances of aeroplanes being in the wrong place such as the Royal Air Force biplane fighter that landed safely in London's Hyde Park or the Avro trainer upside down in somebody's back garden.

The first flying accident I saw was at Ryde Airport in the early 1930s when as a young lad I witnessed an aircraft take off, stall and spin surprisingly slowly into the ground. My father wisely prevented me from running over to look.

The funniest (yes, I know and yes I did say 'funny') accident I saw was during the middle days of the War shortly after we had been 'invaded' by American personnel and equipment. On this particular day, the Home Guard was in training in the fields behind our house at Hatch End near Pinner in Middlesex. They were under the command of a young Army officer and a detachment of real soldiers. The exercise was being conducted with air observation liaison work which was entrusted to an American pilot flying an American Army Piper Cub. I formed the early opinion that this pilot was an accident looking for the right place to happen. He flew in and out of the trees, between the farmer's haystacks and generally put on the sort of display that suggested he was high on testosterone and low on intelligence. In one otherwise innocuous hedgerow there stood a solitary grand and very old world-wise oak tree. It was into its upper branches that the Cub eventually crunched its way to a firm stop. The oak thoughtfully held it tight while the pilot, to the accompaniment of a torrent of surprisingly bad language, fought his way out and shinned down to the ground nursing a torn flying suit and a rather gory knee.

That was amusing enough made the more so by the fact it was an American aeroplane, a bad-tempered American pilot and also that, so far at least, the oak tree had won. But what happened next was pure slapstick. The Cub was only a little bit damaged and looking up at it as you walked round the tree, you could see that it would not have taken too long to repair. The young army officer took charge of the situation and from somewhere secured a rope which he cleverly threw over the tail of the erstwhile flying machine. With a dozen men on each end, he proceeded to order everybody to pull. The oak, seeing its opportunity, quickly let go of the Cub which slid backwards out of the tree landing rudder first on the ground. We watched as the fabric-covered tubular steel fuselage crumpled and the wings fell off. The British Army had succeeded in administering a significant *coup de grace* as the pilot disappeared over the hill in the back of an army jeep, presumably to hospital or at least a comforting bandage.

Too many accidents are due to pilots with exhibitionist tendencies. Unfortunately, showing off is something that most people do when young but happily soon grow out of. But the thought that maturity comes with a pilot's licence is a fallacy and I have seen several examples of crashes caused by somebody trying to impress a friend, usually of the opposite sex. One of these involved a decent enough young chap who had just got his licence on Austers. It was soon after the war and he had bought himself a single-seat racing aircraft of pre-war origin and had it expensively overhauled. He then invited his girlfriend to watch him make his first flight in his valuable, irreplaceable machine. Ten minutes later she was helping drag his bloodstained body out of the wreckage buried in a hedgerow. His wounds were superficial and quickly healed, but the aircraft was a write-off.

And then there was the case of the well-known radio and television broadcaster who hired a Tiger Moth to 'beat up' his girlfriend's country home only to smash into a tree in her garden. He was unhurt, but the Tiger was destroyed. Soon afterwards he approached me to borrow one of my Club machines and was quite offended when I told him that the answer was 'no' in bright letters!

What's the difference between a mishap and an accident? I am afraid I don't know but I'll tell you the tale of my friend, the late Jim McMahon of Crop Culture (Aerial) Ltd. It's a story which has all the characteristics of a West

End farce and was played out successfully without loss of blood or too much pride. Now Jim was an ace crop-spraying pilot. Australian by birth he had flown extensively in his home country, New Zealand and South Africa. He was a good pilot and a responsible one. As director of Crop Culture (Aerial) Ltd, sister company of Britten-Norman Limited at Bembridge, Isle of Wight, he knew his way around things.

While undertaking an agricultural assignment in the West Country one day he had one of those mishaps which was really down to simple bad luck. Landing in long grass he failed to detect a partly concealed tree stump hiding in the vegetation. He struck it with the port lower wing-tip at about touch-down speed, the aircraft swung pretty violently but Jim reacted rapidly and counteracted while at the same time whacking the switches off in case it did a nose-over. The Tiger did indeed stand on its nose but very fortunately the engine had already stopped and the prop was horizontal and unbroken. In fact the Tiger and its flyer were largely unhurt.

The same could not be said of the port lower wing. Those of you who are familiar with the history of the Tiger Moth will know that it was derived directly from the DH.60 Moth which had unstaggered, unswept wings that folded backwards for storage. The Tiger was built using exactly the same castings for the wing fittings but, because it had stagger and sweep-back, the wings could not be folded since, although the rear spar fittings that formed the pivot points in the 60 Moth were the same, they were no longer in vertical alignment.

The blow on the lower wing-tip had pushed the wing backwards, sheared off the rear-spar fitting at the wooden spar and, pivoting about the front-spar attachment, had thrust the wing under the fuselage. Because of the stiff wire bracing between the wings, this had twisted the top wing so that the tip at the leading edge was pointing downwards and the trailing edge upwards.

The telephone rang on my desk. 'Arthur! I've gone and busted up G-Axxx!' It was a rather bad-tempered Jim and it was a Friday morning. 'OK' I responded. 'I know where you are so I'll fly up in the two-seat Tiger [the crop-sprayers, of course, were single-seaters] and collect you'. 'Don't bother', said Jim. 'I think I can fix it and I'll call you back!'

At this stage I didn't know all the details, certainly not that the port rear-spar was detached and the top wing twisted. However, one knew and trusted Jim's experience. At half past three in the afternoon came another call. 'I'm on my way but will be flying low and slow!'

It was just over two hours later that somebody spotted a Tiger Moth flying in very low over Brading Marshes. About a hundred feet high it was – and well throttled back. It was Jim. Gingerly he made a straight-in approach and drove straight onto the grass runway with as delicate a touchdown as one might ever wish for. As he taxied in, it was clear that all was far from well. The lower port wing-tip leading edge was covered in a cut and flattened-out oil can wrapped around the adjacent ribs and held firm with adhesive parcel tape. Holes in the top wing (where Jim had inspected the upper wing spars) were covered over with cardboard liberally affixed with yet more sticky take. But it was the silent crowd of Britten-Norman engineers and staff around the portside rear wing root that witnessed the *pièce de resistance*!

Jim had summoned a local blacksmith and asked him to bring out some strip steel. The only suitable material the smithy had were unbent horseshoes, bars of ribbed iron with square holes in them! The damaged rear-spar root had been exposed and a goodly-sized chunk of Farmers' Union-approved fence-post wired into place and the ends twisted up tightly. This had then been bored (the word 'drilled' somehow seemed unlikely) for some coach bolts which passed through the horseshoe bars and formed a fresh end through which another coach bolt of approximate diameter secured the whole thing to the fuselage spar fitting. The fabric-stripped portion of the wing root, because it was in the slipstream, had been covered with stout agricultural tarpaulin secured at the trailing edge by loops of baling wire that passed right round the wing.

Jim had had a quick look at the wing spars, top and bottom, and saw on their surfaces lines of cracked varnish – a sure sign of 'shakes' where the wood had partially splintered. However, he thought that since the top-wing spars were mostly in compression while flying, he'd be OK so long as he went slowly!

And so Jim had flown some 175 miles with an aircraft held together with baling wire, oil cans, parcel tape and horseshoes! But there was one last good laugh in the whole event. Jim recounted how he had been nervous because the machine did not fly very well and he guessed that the port wing box was moving back and forth due to play in the repaired joints. For this reason he flew as low as he dared over open countryside and with the engine on low throttle, all the time watching for trouble. Suddenly he smelled smoke! Fire! Surely the last thing he had expected to occur! In a moment of panic he selected his field for landing and only then did he see that he had just flown over some chap's garden where he had a good bonfire sending smoke up into his flightpath.

Unfortunately there's a lot of myth and hype about crashes. How often do we read of some poor pilot's last gallant attempt to steer his crashing plane away from a school or a residential estate! Sometimes this may be possible but more often than not the truth is far more prosaic. A pilot in a high speed dice with imminent disaster can't spot the school or the chapel: he's coming down fast and most likely out of control! Nevertheless he'll do his utmost to steer clear of anything hard, be it a school or the local cemetery. He's best off in open land and that he knows. In the sometimes fraction of a second he may have left, the fact is that, nice thought though it is (especially for his poor relatives if he doesn't survive), no, he didn't manage to identify the school and the old people's home as they flashed into his preoccupied view. His natural reaction to avoid flying into anything hard probably saved lives but his reaction would, mostly, have been the instinctive reflex action towards self-preservation. The chances of him being capable of avoiding people on the ground are inevitably very, very slim. Sad fact of life but, nevertheless, fact.

Have you noticed that airliners never really *crash* anywhere these days? It's thought a bit old hat to talk about a 'crash'. But how much richer to have a *plunge*! Yes, an airliner *plunging* into the sea, a ploughed field or a housing estate is much better as regards newsworthiness. 'The crippled aircraft *plunged* out of the sky – but the pilot *wrestled* with the controls to avoid hitting a school below!' Now that is good, sensational popular journalism. However, when we apply the rules established just now we find, to our dismay, that the pilot, as he *wrestled* with his controls (why, we don't know, but we can be certain that they had to be wrestled with) simply didn't give a thought to the 200 passengers behind him, the 400 children on the ground or the newly-painted garden shed of the local vicar that lay dead ahead. No, dear readers! You and I both know he was responding to the oldest sensation in the book – self-preservation and getting his crippled, *plunging* plane down safely.

In many ways we should be glad he was thinking of his own skin rather than concentrating his thoughts on the passengers behind him. After all, he's the one sitting right up front in the cockpit and he's the one whose nose will hit the concrete slab first in a crash. No, we want – yea! *demand* that our airline pilots are schooled in self-preservation for we know that our best guarantee of survival is to hang along behind them! Only when we see the pilot parachute to earth leaving us alone in the sky can we be certain that the system has let us all down badly.

Back in the 1920s, some passenger-carrying aircraft were built in which the pilot sat way back along the fuselage and closer to fin than wing. I'd have been a bit uncertain flying along with a guy sitting so far back that by the time his part of the aeroplane stopped in a crash my end would have been compressed into a dead-passenger-rich soup of splinters and torn fabric!

I repeat, aircraft crashes are not in the slightest bit funny. But just occasionally there's a set of circumstances that has us in laughter. I remember as a boy seeing a comedy film where a number of crew escaped from an allegedly doomed plane (I think it was some time before aircraft had started plunging, though) and they all jumped with parachutes. One of the crew got hooked up in a tree by his parachute cords and, well-suspended, was slowly rotating in circles. His other crew mates ran to his tree, looked up at him and said 'Where's the pilot?' To which the gyrating airman said 'Over there!' and raised a pointing hand that quickly encompassed 360 degrees of horizon.

That, of course, was a film. Allow me to relate a real and much more recent incident with a funny outcome. About four years ago the young unfortunate pilot of a very expensive RAF high-speed jet fighter who was on a training exercise suffered some sort of terminal systems failure from which there was never going to be a cheerful ending. Accordingly, and as trained, he fired his ejection seat as his crippled, *plunging* jet scythed through some power cables of the National Grid and exploded in a farm paddock. Shocked but safe, he settled unharmed in a field of vegetables right outside the farmhouse from which emerged a genuinely concerned lady for whom the well-being of the erstwhile flyer was paramount in her thoughts.

"You poor young man!" she said as she helped him to his feet. "Come into the farmhouse and sit down. I'd offer to make you a cup of tea only the electric's just gone off for some reason…"

When we learn to fly we are always told that if we don't like our landing, open up and go round again. If you bounce on landing, bang open the throttle and make for the skies again. Like all rules, though, there are exceptions and in flying training somebody ought to remember to teach those exceptions. Take the tale of the day back in the immediate post-war years when my local flying club decided to attend a distant air rally organised by another club. It was an ideal exercise for those of our members who were newly-qualified and for all of us an opportunity to hone our navigation skills. The story concerns one particular member who was a friend of mine. He had just qualified for his Private Pilot's Licence and was anxious to demonstrate his prowess at taming the skies to his young lady.

It was a Saturday morning and with a good forecast except for a bit of mist near our destination, a whole bunch of light aircraft set off in raggle-taggle formation – Auster Autocrats, Taylorcrafts and Miles Magisters. My young friend and his lady were in a brand new Auster. Naturally, none of us carried radio.

As the flight proceeded in a westerly direction, visibility grew steadily worse – far worse than forecast – and soon we were in real, genuine fog and low cloud. It was getting hairy and the fellow upon whom I had formated gestured that he was turning back. There's always the nagging doubt that an unnecessary flight taking unnecessary risks is unnecessarily risky and it is better to be safe and fly another day. I, too, turned for home and soon realised that of the six or seven machines in our bunch, at least four were headed back. My young friend was not one of them.

Now picture his predicament. Here he was in a brand new club aeroplane with his brand new girlfriend and in his pocket a brand new pilot's licence. With the inexperience of the neophyte, he decided to press on but after a few moments finally realised his mistake. Below was a small but adequate field. He quickly went through all the correct procedures, lined up on the meadow and prepared for his first-ever genuine forced landing. Always taught never to undershoot, he came over the hedge high and touched down well into the small field – only to bounce! His instinct, honed at the knee of a good Club instructor, was to go round again and have another go. So he shoved the throttle hard forward, whereupon he went into the far hedge at high speed, breaking his new aeroplane and causing fortunately only minor injuries to himself and his passenger. The exception has to be that when landing in a very small field, if you bounce, better to hold it and risk a broken undercarriage rather than a broken aeroplane! His predicament understood, his mishap was forgiven by the Club instructor – and later we all went to his wedding!

If accidents are gruesome, almost all are spectacular. They range from the British European Airways' DC-3 which departed Northolt in a blizzard and heavy icing conditions and landed atop a pair of houses less than a mile away, to the pilot of a microlight which descended on top of a marquee in the grounds of a country house where a garden party was taking place. The pilot was invited to join in and had a thoroughly enjoyable afternoon with his new-found friends while his flying machine was carefully lifted down by several young guests and the marquee hiring company was advised that the holes in their tent must have been caused by overnight moths.

In the famous DC-3 accident, it is reported that the Dakota completely removed the roofs of a pair of semi-detached houses as it came to a halt perched on top of the walls. When the mayhem had stabilised, the crew and their solitary passenger climbed out of the fuselage, opened the attic trap-door and dropped down into the upstairs landing to make their way down the stairs and out through the front door.

A well-known test pilot had a terrible mishap in the 1950s, crashing a prototype aircraft onto a golf course. In shock, injured and bleeding, he was gallantly rescued by the club secretary who took him straight into the members' bar while he summoned an ambulance. As he sat trembling with the aftermath of his experience and downing a welcome brandy, two club members came in and were heard to say in a loud voice 'Who's that scruffy feller? Shouldn't be in here dressed like that and bleedin' all over the place! Jolly bad form!"

Crashes in time of war are generally depressing images of Man's intolerance against his fellow Man. I had a personal insight into the stupidity of it all very early on in the war when I was still at college. Yes, we had all been through the blitz and yes, along with many others, our family home was damaged by a too-close HE bomb.

Near where we lived a German bomber engaged in a weekend daylight raid had been badly shot up. He was far from home and faced little chance of going anywhere but downwards. His destiny proved to lie in a newly-cut hayfield into which he crash-landed, wheels up, one engine pouring black smoke and generally looking non-airworthy. What happened next was quite amazing. From this 'stockbroker's belt' area of well-to-do residents emerged a rabble of men who, by virtue of their presence, suggested they were excluded military service meaning they were doctors, bank managers and similar bastions of the community. Now, armed with whatever garden tool they could grab, they rabble-ran into the fields clearly hell-bent on some sort of revenge.

By mere virtue of proximity, I was first on the scene and already had a tentative hand on the erstwhile enemy's wing-tip as the young pilot clad in white flying overalls, opened his cockpit canopy and prepared for a quick and understandable exit from something that looked as if it would blow up at any moment. He looked straight at me and I caught sight of his eyes. The first thing I saw was that he was little more than my age – a young man in the prime of youth. The other thing I saw was the look of terror in his face as the crowd of local ruffians advanced, shouting and screaming and banging their weapons on his poor plane. The young fellow quickly retreated into his cockpit and sat there as white as his overalls but wisely leaving the hood open.

The local self-proclaimed militia encircled the wreck and continued to shout and make threatening gestures while the pilot cowered in his cockpit. In the distance there appeared a corpulent police constable of the old sort so familiarly portrayed by cartoonists as ruddy-faced and rotund. Mounted on an elderly police pushbike he unsteadily bounced his way across the field until he drew level with the Dornier where he dismounted and looked around. The rabble fell silent, one man pointing his spear (a garden hoe) at the cockpit and muttering loudly. Still one of the engines belched smoke but didn't quite appear to be on fire.

Officer Plod leaned his bike against the front of the battered wing, walked slowly round the engine and wing tip to the trailing edge which was flat on the ground – and walked up onto the wing. He said something to the pilot. We didn't hear what it was but it was probably something like 'I arrest you for landing an unairworthy foreign plane in a newly-harvested British hay field.' Whatever it was, the young fellow stood up, stepped out, followed the officer off the wing onto the ground and round to his bicycle. Pushing his bike in one hand, and holding the German flyer by the arm with the other, the two set off to walk across the field. The rabble grudgingly parted and let them through. My feeling was that the lad was so grateful for the calm and mature presence of authority that he was only too willing to be 'arrested' although I am sure if he had really wanted to he could have easily slipped the portly officer's grip. Had he done so I suspect he would have been shredded by the throng. As it was he must have been relieved to be alive and protected from the local community.

I went back next day to try to photograph the aircraft but, amazingly, it had gone, only the tracks of heavy-wheeled vehicles suggesting that it had been salvaged during the night. We never heard any more of the young airman.

Crashes and prangs clearly come in all shapes and sizes. The causes of their transformation into so much scrap (or an expensive rebuild) are many and surprisingly varied. Some aircraft, for instance, can crash without ever leaving the ground – and even attain this conclusion with engines not just stopped but still stone cold! A case in point was the celebrated Avro Anson. Here's what I mean.

The original Anson was the wooden winged Avro 12 which had a hand-retracted undercarriage – performing something like 500 turns of a handwheel while trying to hold steady in the climb was never easy. The more refined metal Avro 19, however, was much better. Here undercarriage retraction was hydraulic. In the rather confined space between the two cockpit seats was a plunger rather like the top of a fire extinguisher. It was held down by a spring-loaded claw catch at the aft side. To retract the wheels, all you had to do was slide the locking catch back with the thumb – and the plunger would come up all by itself, the wheels following suit. Lowering them meant pushing the plunger back down whereupon the spring-loaded claw lock automatically held it down.

This was fine and gave one a sense of power. There was only one drawback to the system. In getting out of the cockpit with flying boots on it was all too easy to kick off that safety catch without even knowing. Whereupon up came the plunger and so did the wheels. Or, rather more noticeably, down went the aeroplane. It was thus embarrassing to fly to your destination, taxi in smartly, park in line with aplomb, switch off the engines – and then retract your wheels. The design boffins thought long and hard about this and came up with a solution! Simply re-position the locking lever so that, instead of being at the back of the plunger and kickable when you left your seat, it was at the front where kicking it on the way out would have no effect.

Ansons were modified throughout the Royal Air Force. Shortly afterwards, somebody about to start a flight, climbed carelessly into his seat – and kicked the catch. The aircraft immediately settled on its wood-framed canvas-covered belly and array of underneath aerials. It was not a pretty sound! Eventually somebody twigged that if you put the catch on one side instead of front or back, no matter which way you were going you could not kick the undercarriage up! Simple thing but it proved expensive to sort out.

A friend and fellow lightplane flier was Arthur J 'Bill' Pegg, chief test pilot for Bristol Aeroplane Company. On February 4th 1954 he was flying a brand-new Britannia airliner G-ALRX when he experienced a small mid-air fire in an engine bay. With increasingly complicated control problems and power failure he made an absolutely copybook forced landing. The only problem was that it was in the low-water mud of the Severn Estuary at Littleton Wharf. He waded ashore but the aeroplane was immovable and he (and his bosses) had to watch as the incoming tide left nothing but the tip of the tall fin showing. We had just broken our Club Miles Magister, so we sent him a telegram of condolences…

I mentioned earlier that I had had one or two mishaps of my own. One of the most peculiar was while I was flying not as pilot but as a passenger in a British European Airways' Vickers Viscount to Rome. It concluded with a memorable telephone call to my father who knew that I was on that particular flight. 'Hello, Dad! I've been in a bit of a plane crash and I'm still at Heathrow but I'm OK.'

It was Sunday, January 16th 1955 and I was on my way for an early Monday morning meeting in Rome. Armed with my ticket I boarded a three-year-old Viscount 701 at London's Heathrow Airport together with around 30 or so other passengers. It had been a particularly raw start to the New Year with a big freeze with blizzards, then a thaw with heavy flooding followed by dense fog and it was in these marginal visibility conditions that I took my seat in this, one of the last of the big-windowed passenger planes to be built. At this period in its colourful existence, Heathrow was still being developed and was dotted with building sites.

In due course the engines started and the aircraft taxied out. As a flyer myself I was understandably apprehensive especially as quite quickly the last visible airport building vanished into the murk. Still we taxied slowly forward until there was a sharp turn as we lined up for take-off. A pause – and then full power. The machine surged forward and I peered out of the big oval window to see whatever there was to see. All at once I caught a glimpse of a yellow digger and buildings and then there was an immense impact as the airliner struck something pretty solid at an estimated 100 miles an hour and spun round 180 degrees shedding large and expensive bits on the way.

It was a while before everybody got themselves together and scrambled out to find that we were well and truly in a builders' storage area. In the murk, the pilot had confused the turn-off to the active runway and instead lined up on an abandoned runway that was now under expansion. The runway we were supposed to be on was 200 yards further on. For the time being, we had succeeded in levelling a workman's hut and the site workshop as well as the staff canteen wagon, striking concrete blocks, piles of steel mesh and a mountain of aggregate for making concrete. The concrete mixer itself had narrowly escaped the attention of our runaway aircraft.

Almost immediately, and before we rather shaken passengers were taken into care, a BEA team arrived and, revealing a nifty touch of the hagiocracy associated with airliners and mishaps, quickly black-painted out the name 'British European Airways' on both sides of the plane. Nice touch, that, for it proves that when the crash alarm sounds, the response is not just fire engine, crash tender and ambulance, but the fellow with the job of obliterating the blindingly obvious because, sure as little eggs, the newspapers will sooner or later find out the operator of the airliner that has just crashed!

Miraculously on that occasion nobody was hurt and even the aeroplane, described in one newspaper as a '£250,000 plane wrecked beyond repair', was rebuilt and saw some further years in service. I, though, missed my meeting while I expect others had their plans disturbed, too. But there was one final twist to this tale of Captain Eric Wait's forgettable day that renders this tale a candidate for the 'funny prang' file – the runaway Viscount was registered G-AMOK!

As I hope I have shown, very few commercial aircraft accidents are anywhere approaching comedy. But there was one exception where afterwards everybody had a good laugh. On August 15th 1967 Channel Airways' HS.748 G-ATEK from Jersey was approaching Portsmouth Airport. The grass surface was soaking wet with dew as the two-year old turbo-jet made a normal touch-down. The problem arose when the captain applied the brakes. Nothing happened! The aeroplane sailed across the airfield and zoinged through the chain mesh fence onto the busy main road where it stopped miraculously without causing a vehicle crash or injuring anybody. The local newspaper quickly got a number of telephone calls and despatched its reporter pronto.

About two hours later, a second Channel Airways' HS.748 from Jersey, this one G-ATEH, was approaching Portsmouth and the Control Tower alerted the pilot to the presence of both wet conditions and a hole in the fence through which his company's previous flight had just been dragged back. The captain landed as usual, put on the brakes – and nothing happened! The aircraft sailed across the grass, &c, &c. The local newspaper office started getting fresh telephone calls. 'There's an aeroplane gone through the fence onto the main road!' 'Yes, Yes', came the rather bored response. 'We've already got that story. Thank you very much!'

The sad aspect of that story (in which nobody was seriously hurt and both aeroplanes were quickly repaired) was that it led to the closure of that fine grass aerodrome beloved by a generation of south coast fliers.

Occasionally one may court disaster! In the 1950s Denham was popular with movie-makers and dramas involving aeroplanes, espionage and police chases were in their infancy. An epic was being filmed at the airfield on one occasion. The plot had criminals starting up an aeroplane and taking off as the police car turned in their path. The wheel of the aircraft strikes the car, the aircraft gets airborne but has no power and crashes into trees.

To make this, the film people bought a brand new Auster for the flying shots and also got Austers to make a flyable replica which they could crash. The people at Rearsby co-operated fully and to everybody's amazement there appeared two identical aircraft at Denham each with the same registration – G-AGTS! The duplicate was an old condemned fuselage frame and a pair of old ex-army Auster wings. The engine was a block of concrete with a projection to pivot an old propeller. Everything else looked OK but was all built of scrap components.

At this point, let's talk about the film as it was shot. The dummy Auster, fitted out with a large and expensive movie camera (there were no small video cameras in those days) in the cockpit, was towed into the air by the other Auster, the camera running. Then it was released and the camera recorded the aircraft gliding down until it struck the trees and dived into the ground. It was all done very realistically and looked authentic enough.

Unseen from the movie-goer was the parallel problems of shooting the rest of the film. The real Auster was being poled around the sky for the cameras when it misjudged height and position – and hit the ground very hard! With collapsed undercarriage, bent cowlings and a one-and-a-half-blade propeller it was out of filming for a long while. The film producers' adage about never working with children and animals was duly amended to include aeroplanes!

By the nature of the beast, the majority of crashes involving modern tin jet-powered aircraft tend to leave behind little that is recognisable – an evil blackening of earth and a few gruesome pieces of mangled iron and only the imagination with which to visualise the final moments of blind terror. For that reason the greater majority of my pictures are from a past era when more identifiable remains survived. The first fifty years of flying afforded us more pictorial reminders than, unfortunately, more recent times. Light aircraft, inter-war Royal Air Force machines and some First War veterans in curious situations were photogenic and there were usually some lessons to be learned from studying the damage. There are exceptions and a few more recent prangs are included.

By far the greater majority of these images are of British aircraft although some are pictured a long way from home. In general, the pictures are arranged chronologically wherever possible. Again where information exists the events they portray are accurately dated and the accident described. Mind you, not all of my pictures were professionally taken so, amidst top quality photographic press agency and newspaper pictures expect to find some pretty rough amateur snapshots. They were taken by people who were in the right (or wrong) place at the right time and hence we should be thankful for an image, however ill-exposed, poorly composed and badly printed it may be. Cameras were not all that common and, in those days, portable telephones didn't exist. Even when they did they were not used for taking pictures! ... Enough chit-chat: let's get on with the pictures!

Designed by the Royal Aircraft Factory, the BE.2c was one of the RFC's early workhorse aeroplanes. But even the most commonly-used machines came a cropper and here is a Vickers-built example, 5434, pictured after spinning in at Filton in 1912. The slow-flying and stable BE.2c was widely deployed in France during the War but was such easy prey for Richtofen's *Jasta* that one diarist reported 'no-man's land carpeted with wrecked BEs'. Of course it took many young lives, too.

During the middle of the First World War, flying training was still being undertaken on Henry Farman F.20 pushers. The Grahame-White Aviation Co Ltd at Hendon built a batch of 100 of these including this one, A1210, which sustained this mishap in the winter of 1917. Note that the prefix 'A', while appearing on the tail, is elided from the number painted on the nose of the fuselage nacelle. Despite this tangle of parts, even crashed aircraft worse than this were usually repairable and this example was back in the air in less than a week.

Besides the BE series of aircraft, another product of the Royal Aircraft Factory at South Farnborough was the RE.8. It was one of the more unhappy aircraft of the First World War era. Despite some unfortunate problems including what at the time was described as 'spiral instability', more than 3,800 were built by several contractors. And 2,000 were used on the Western Front by nearly every corps squadron where they were used for artillery observation. It was easily damaged and easily repaired but at the cost of stability. After a while, like so many contemporary aircraft, the Raftight-coated fabric eventually went soggy and limp, the rigging went awry and tailplanes warped. Sombrely, Hugh Trenchard had declared in 1917 that no RE.8 was to be repaired where the lower longeron 'was out' meaning broken. Dubbed the 'Harry Tate' after a popular music hall figure of the time, the RE.8 was not popular with ground crew because it was tricky to rig correctly and the joke was that it had dihedral in both directions, for the nose appeared to point upwards. It was even more unpopular with pilots, one of whom said it 'killed them more easily than it did the test and delivery pilots at home'. Its proneness to spin without warning usually crumpled the 48-gallon petrol tank releasing its contents onto the red-hot engine exhaust pipes. It even raised questions in the House, MP Noel Pemberton-Billing complaining 'I am informed it is not an easy machine to fly and that it requires the skill of an experienced pilot' – the very pilots that did not exist in RFC squadrons. Eventually the aircraft found a major role in training and in this work it acquired a larger tail fin to improve the stall/spin recovery procedure. The machine pictured here, C2441, was one of a batch of 850 built in Coventry by Daimler. It appears to have had a mishap at the back of a hangar: note the presence of the high-tech recovery vehicle and its attendant labour force at the left.

Although the maximum speed was alleged to be 102 mph, the time taken for the RE.8 to climb to 6,500 feet at 340 ft/minute was a quarter of an hour and to 10,000 feet a massive 29 minutes. Ponderous in the air, it was all too easy fodder for enemy fliers and also for Ack-Ack guns. This unidentified example, bearing the name *Gadget* painted under its cockpit, is displaying the under-wing bomb-racks used by attack versions. There appears to be one 20lb Cooper bomb hung-up under each wing.

Generally speaking, when early aeroplanes hit obstructions such as trees, the trees remained intact and only the machine gets broken. Here is an exception to the rule where an oak tree has suffered grievous damage at the wings of an AirCo DH.6 of No. 49 TDS (Training Depot Station) Royal Flying Corps at South Carlton, Lincolnshire which was the HQ of 23rd Wing Royal Flying Corps. While the name of the pilot and the date of the incident remain unrecorded (possibly a blessing for the erstwhile young flyer who perpetrated this high-grade super-prang), it is known that this mishap occurred somewhere near his base at Catterick in September 1918 by which time, of course, he would have been in the Royal Air Force. Contemporary accounts speak of this as 'one of the many similar training incidents' of the time which does suggest that being a tree anywhere near such an establishment must have been a highly dangerous occupation – for a tree, that is. Quite early on in Service flying training it is usually instilled in the trainee that trees should be avoided at all costs. Curious, then, that so many nascent flyers seem to end up in them, on them or simply wrapped around them.

Another training accident, this time to a BE.2c which suffered a more prosaic and spectacular accident when it misjudged a forced landing and became entangled in one of the multiple arrays of telephone wires that once embellished our railway lines. Here a salvage crew is contemplating what to do next. A similar but different view of this same scene appears in Alan Morris's book *Bloody April* (Jarrold, 1967) about the youthful pilots in the RFC and the trials and tribulations of their training.

So long as the aeroplane held together during its descent, the allegedly primitive aeroplanes that we used in the First World War offered a good chance of survival in an accident. Here an unidentified Airco DH.6 has undergone an inverted landing in a ditch against an earth bank and hedgerow. The fuselage has broken through at the rear seat attachment frame yet pilot and observer were able to crawl out with minimal injury. A key problem at the time was that full cockpit harness was still a long way in the future and most machines merely had a lap-strap to hold the pilot in during manoeuvres. This was fine but if the machine stopped suddenly as it did in this case, there was little to prevent ingestion of instruments and repositioned facial features.

DH.6 B2762 was one of a batch of 500 aircraft built by the Aircraft Manufacturing Company Ltd at Hendon during the First World War. This was an age when if an aircraft crashed, whatever it hit was usually far less damaged than the aeroplane and this is a case in point. For some forgotten reason, the pilot managed to strike the corner timbers supporting the outriggers for the hangar doors. They have survived undamaged but the aeroplane looks somewhat the worse for wear in this snapshot from an unidentified airfield in 1917. It is doubtful that this aircraft ever flew again.

Many were the examples of Avro 504K aircraft in our skies. First used in the Great War, they were still flying well into the 1930s using a variety of engines. This one, however, wasn't. One of a batch of 500 built by A V Roe at the end of the conflict, H2482 spun in from a great height and was, in the words of the Maintenance Unit, 'reduced to produce', never to fly again.

Talk today of the Sopwith Scout and few people will know what you're on about. Yet this was, originally, the official name of the famous Sopwith Pup single seat scout/fighter. Beautiful to fly, simple and light to manoeuvre, the Pup's low wing-loading gave it aerobatic performance in excess of 15,000 feet while it could be landed accurately in the smallest space. Famously used for balloon-strafing in the Battle of Arras by the RFC and pioneering deck-landing for the RNAS, the Pup was devoid of all vices. Except, perhaps, pilots. Although marked 7313, this machine is actually A7313, one of a batch built by The Standard Motor Co Ltd of Coventry. The picture shows that the machine has landed amidst a stack of ladders and drainpipes in an airfield's maintenance section. Apart from a bent undercarriage and a shortened lower starboard mainplane, this particular example of the 1,313 machines built looks repairable.

There's a class of man who has been around for hundreds of years. He's the one who likes to pose with his conquest. The hunter with a foot on some poor wretched dead animal, the salvers of the shipwreck and so on. Flying encouraged this sort of behaviour and, certainly in the First World War, if you shot down your enemy it was quite respectable to land next to the wreck and have your photo taken with it. And if it was your own crash, well, it was just as photogenic! This snapshot comes from 1917 and shows a downed Avro with a retracted undercarriage and some of the front missing. But it is a good excuse for a photo. Unfortunately the place and the circumstances are not recorded, nor is the identity of the particular machine.

The most frequent landing accident to early aircraft was the nose-over. Tall undercarriages which raised the engine thrust-line, narrow wheels that sank into soft ground, uneven airfield surfaces and variable piloting techniques all contributed to the rash of aircraft found standing on their noses not only on landing but on take-off and even while taxiing. When conducted at speed, the nose-over developed into a full-blown inverted position. Some aircraft, such as the BE.2e A2822 seen here, seldom went completely over, the aircraft geometry combining with the weight of the engine to keep the machine standing on top wing and propeller. Ground crews had to learn the correct technique for righting aircraft from these positions and doing it without causing more damage. Generally a pair of shear-legs would be used to raise the tail while a restraining rope with another pair of shear-legs would gently lower the aircraft back the right way up. Here ropes are being tied around the rear fuselage prior to a lift.

While the BE.2 series was usually suited to an inverted landing with minimal damage, other machines were often less successful at this manoeuvre. Here is Bristol Scout 8991 which overturned at East Fortune, near Haddington, Scotland, on May 23rd 1917. Nobody was injured although the shape of the top wings suggests that they at least never flew again.

This DH.4 B7747 overran on landing after a test flight during which incorrect rigging was determined. It ended up crossing a sunken road and striking a hedge and ditch at Bellevue Aerodrome in France. The date was February 16th 1918 and the pilot, standing left by the cockpit, was the renowned Alan H Curtiss. Next to him is his observer, 2nd Lt V Gordon. The fact that the propeller is unbroken – as far as the uppermost blades are concerned, suggests the engine had already stopped before the aircraft followed suit.

Sam Saunders opened his boat-building yard at East Cowes and built several pioneering flying boats before being taken over by A V Roe and becoming the well-known Saunders-Roe business. During the First World War his business was one of the many aircraft construction contractors. In the 1916 allocations his firm built a batch of 50 Avro 504 aircraft, some as 504A (80 hp Gnome engine) and others as the more powerful 504J with the 100 hp Gnome Monosoupape. A9798 appears to be a J although after this heavy landing it was no doubt reduced to spares.

Amongst the very first aircraft ordered by the newly-formed Royal Air Force in April 1918 was a batch of 500 Avro 504K aircraft from A V Roe & Company. This one, E3648, has met with a training accident and come to grief. Interestingly, this machine had variable-incidence tailplane gear which has broken in the impact allowing the whole tailplane to droop.

In 1918, the newly-founded Royal Air Force also ordered 250 Sopwith 1F.1 Camel fighters which were built in Norwich by Boulton & Paul Ltd. This one, F1343, was test-flown at No. 5 (AFC) Minchampton on June 8th 1918 by Alan Curtiss who found that it was very tail heavy and that the wing bracing wires were vibrating badly – a sign that they were too slack. On approach to land, the Camel took command of the situation, struck hard and turned over. The conclusion was that it was badly rigged. Despite the undignified return to its base it was repaired.

A remarkable series of tiny snapshots found in an abandoned album belonging to a one-time RAF fitter reveals the problems of flying Handley Page O/400 bombers during the First World War when they had but elemental instruments. These machines had no accurate airspeed indicators nor attitude indicators meaning that it was all too easy to stall on the climb-out from take-off. Furthermore, the tail assemblies were prone to extreme mechanical vibration which could initiate aerodynamic flutter. Accidents to the big Handley Pages were far from uncommon but it was a fluke that the person who took these shots actually portrayed a crash sequence and its aftermath. The first picture shows the aircraft climbing away on take-off. From the ground it is easy to see that the tail is low.

In this second picture, the aircraft has stalled and is falling to the ground – a split second from impact. What the picture cannot show is that despite the huge bulk of these aircraft, stalling and spinning, while difficult to control, was actually a remarkably slow affair. Test reports on the O/400 give an established spin rate of one rotation of about 4.5 seconds with a recovery of half to one full turn depending on axis of spin. These are almost sedate rates of descent.

The third picture I have selected from the eight images of this event shows the aircraft after it has hit the ground. While the front is stove in and the undercarriage pushed well backwards, the integrity of the bulk of the structure is preserved – a truly remarkable and unexpected outcome.

The final image I have chosen is a close-up of the starboard side showing the wheels forced back under the wings. The impression is that the pilot may have not survived this impact even though his aircraft is surprisingly intact. I have no further details on these pictures, not even where the event happened. The date is around 1918 and the location may be overseas.

No 216 Squadron was formed in January 1918 at Ochey, France, and had a mixed assortment of aircraft ranging from the DH.10 to the Handley Page O/400, Vickers Vimy and later an assortment of Victorias, Valencias and Vernons. The big Handley Pages were large and reliable but they had one disturbing characteristic that, curiously, plagued the much later HP.42 airliners of the 1930s. This was that it was not easy to judge the angle of climb or level flight attitude. With a paucity of instruments, it was only experience and a degree of intuition that told when you were flying straight and level or, more importantly, whether you were climbing at the safe angle for airspeed. This is why a common cause of O/400 crashes was the stall and spin situation. Here we see 216's C9685 following a slow-speed spin while engaged on a mail flight. The accident happened on February 12th 1919 at Geyen. Interestingly this shows that the aircraft's serial number was painted on the underside of both wings, both sides of the rear fuselage and on the underside!

One of the oldest RFC and later RAF Squadrons was Number 12 founded in February 1915 at Netheravon and, after the end of WWI, it was based at Bickendorf, Germany. It was near here in 1919 that Lt McQueen experienced a problem with his Bristol F.2B Fighter H1594, descending in an undignified heap next to a railway line – note the signal just behind the aircraft appropriately showing 'danger'.

Handley Page entered the commercial aircraft business in 1919 with civil conversions of his wartime bombers. G-EANV was the first of a second batch of two O/7 machines modified for the cross-channel service and gained its C of A on October 2nd 1919. The following month it was shipped to Johannesburg and, renamed *Pioneer*, it flew emblazoned with the name of a local brandy – Commando. Used for aerial advertising over Johannesburg, its career was short-lived for on February 22nd 1920 while flying at a height of 300 feet and with a full load of passengers it developed tailplane flutter causing the port rudder post to spring out of its bearing socket. This initiated a very slow but unrecoverable spin which was sustained until the machine struck the ground at Acacia Siding, a settlement near Beaufort West in Cape Province. All ten people on board survived the impact but the Cricklewood-built bomber was a write-off.

The Sopwith T.1 Cuckoo was designed as a torpedo-carrying landplane with folding wigs to allow operation from shore stations or from the nascent aircraft carriers then being experimented with. The Cuckoo was a late project being evaluated at the Isle of Grain in July 1917. First production orders went out the following month but of the 350 ordered, only 90 were confirmed delivered by the time the war end called a stop to manufacture. Unlike other Sopwith types, the Cuckoo was thought an important adjunct to the peacetime Services and so did not make it onto the surplus market as did other designs. This particular example, N8003, was built by Blackburn Aeroplane & Motor Co Ltd as one of a batch of 100 of which only 32 were delivered in 1919. It was used by Nunber 1 Training Flight, 210 squadron at Gosport in 1921. This incident happened on June 6th 1922 as a result of engine failure on take-off. The 'crow's-foot' training-edge fairings for wing-folding are clearly visible on the upper wings behind the inner rear interplane strut attachment points.

Powered by a 436 hp Bristol Jupiter IV radial, the 29-foot span Parnall Plover biplane was a single-seat carrier-borne naval fighter which could be either a landplane or, when fitted with floats, an amphibian. The intention was to create a replacement for the obsolete Nieuport Nightjar. Only a small number were built and their success was limited in favour of the rival Fairey Flycatcher, built to the same 1922 Air Ministry Specification 6/22. This example, N9704, suffered structural failure of the top wing centre-section at the conclusion of a series of unauthorised aerobatic manoeuvres. The pilot, on  a supposedly routine test flight from RAF Leuchars in Fife, was considerably fortunate in surviving the subsequent inverted spin into moorland and the Plover presented an unfamiliar heap of bits to tax the wits of local aircraft spotters of which, in that part of the world, there probably weren't any!

The de Havilland DH.34 was the outcome of systematic developments in biplane commercial aircraft that could be traced back to the first civilianised DH.9a. Through the DH.16 and 18, the Stag Lane company honed its skills to achieve the large and comfortable Model 34 which saw service with Instone and Daimler Hire. With two pilots and enclosed accommodation for nine passengers seated comfortably in wickerwork seats, the DH.34 was the last word in luxury for the time and it successfully plied the cross-channel routes to Brussels and Paris from May 1922 forwards. Powered by one 450 hp Napier Lion, the aircraft had one fault – a high landing speed due to a high wing-loading. In October of 1922, Daimler extended its Croydon to Amsterdam route to travel as far as Manchester. All went well until September 14th 1923 when G-EBBS, pictured here, was destroyed in an attempted forced landing near Ivinghoe Beacon in Buckinghamshire. Attributed to a stall due to the high landing speed, both pilots were killed together with the three passengers on board. The rest of the fleet was modified to take wings of slightly greater area and span which helped reduce the stalling speed. For pilots G E Pratt and Leslie George Robinson it was a bit too late.

George Handasyde was one of the most important of the pioneer designers and his partnership with Helmuth Paul Martin resulted in the famous Woking-based firm of Martinsyde. The WWI F.4 fighter was developed into the amazing Martinsyde Semiquaver racer. Powered by a 300 hp Hispano-Suiza, it set up a new world speed record on March 21st 1920 achieving 161.434 mph over one kilometre at Martlesham Heath. The Fifth Aerial Derby was staged on July 24th, the course being 200 miles comprising two laps of 100 miles each starting from Hendon and taking in Brooklands, Epsom, West Thurrock, Epping, Hertford and thence back to Hendon. Among the fifteen starters was the red Semiquaver which was supposed to be piloted by F P Raynham but a last moment change put the renowned Frank Courtney into the cockpit. In fact only fourteen machines took off, one subsequently crashed and four retired for one reason or another. Nine entrants finished, the outright winner being Courtney in the Semiquaver who had averaged 153.45 miles an hour. Unfortunately, the victory was slightly tarnished when the 'hot' Martinsyde turned over on landing. Courtney was unhurt and the £500 first prize easily covered the cost of repairs.

Developed from the Vickers Commercial airliner, itself descended from the WWI Vimy bomber, the Vickers Vernon was the first aircraft to be designed specifically for troop-carrying duties. It entered service in 1922 and between then and the final batch ordered in November 1924 some 60 examples were built. Most saw service in Iraq where it was found that the original Rolls-Royce Eagle engines, mounted mid-way between the wings, were underpowered in the arid climate. Replaced with 450 hp Napier Lion II engines mounted on top of the lower wing, the machine became a practical and valuable work-horse with Nos 45 and 70 Squadron at Hinaidi. In 1923 this unidentified Vernon was engaged in night-flying trials when it collided with a searchlight on landing. This snapshot taken the following morning shows the recovery attempts in action. Both sides of the undercarriage have collapsed, the remains piled under the nose and the port four-blader has struck something fairly solid while in motion. Undernose damage suggests that the machine attempted a nose-stand before falling back. Field repairs like this were extremely difficult and often accidents like this – which were not uncommon – necessitated dismantling and difficult ground transport back to base workshops.

Built by Short Brothers at Rochester, this Felixstowe flying boat was from a batch of 50 ordered in 1916. Last of the batch, finished in 1918, was N4049 built as a Model F.5 fitted with two Rolls-Royce Eagle VII engines each of 325 hp. Spanning 103 feet 8 inches, these were huge machines and they remained in service into the mid 1920s by which time their duties were restricted to flying boat training. This was undertaken by 480 Flight at Calshot. On November 4th 1924, engine failure caused N4049 to force-land off Portland Bill. Fortunately the light cruiser HMS *Weymouth*, veteran of the First War, was close by and able to rescue the five-man crew seen in this picture taken from the rescue ship on the top wing of their doomed craft. There is a postscript to this event for, on January 10th that same year and in these same waters HMS *Resolution*, returning from exercises with the Mediterranean Fleet, struck and sank the British submarine L.24 without knowing. Some 43 lives were lost on that occasion.

Vickers Virginias were prone to undercarriage problems and, although developed from the robust Vimy bomber, anything other than a good touchdown risked either pulling tyres off or a total collapse. Here we see J6857 of No 7 Squadron at Bircham Newton, with rather more than lost wheels for the nose has also suffered in this mishap. An engine caught fire on November 20th 1924 and in the subsequent forced landing at Bishops Stortford the machine ran into a tree as seen in this picture. The machine was subsequently rebuilt – in fact it was rebuilt several times after various mishaps – before emerging as a Virginia Mk. VII

Accidents can happen to anybody anywhere. Here is an Egyptian Air Force DH.9A ER928 in which P/O Masser-Bennett inverted himself at Abu Sueir in January 1925. Nobody was badly hurt but the wings have developed a curious shape.

Here's one to confuse historians! Marked clearly J711, this DH.9A is actually a scrap rebuild by the RAF Packing Depot at Ascot and was allocated to 207 Squadron at Bircham Newton. On April 30th 1925 while formation flying it apparently lost power from its 400 hp Liberty engine and spun into the ground. The original snapshot is annotated on the reverse 'J7112'.

The broken cockpit of the DH.9A J7112 showing the paucity of instrumentation available to pilots – an altimeter and an engine speed indicator. That pilots attempted flying in cloud and at night with such little in the way of cockpit aids is a wonder – and it is no small wonder that accidents were so numerous.

The Hawker Woodcock II was never a proper 'civil' aircraft but when it was decided to take one on a Scandinavian sales tour preceded by participating in the King's Cup Race in 1925, J7515 was allocated civil markings G-EBMA on July 1st that year. The race started on July 3rd and the Woodcock was flown by Hawker test pilot Major Paul Ward Spencer Bulman. There were fifteen entrants for the 1,608-mile race but on the day persistent and dense fog dogged the event. Perhaps in the circumstances it was not surprising that only three finished the gruelling course. The Woodcock was not among them, though, for on the first day Bulman got lost north of London and attempted a precautionary landing at Luton. It didn't go according to plan and, after striking trees, Bulman was lucky to escape unhurt. The Woodcock didn't.

Vickers responded to a request to tender for the design of a long-range bomber in April 1920 and this heralded the family of bomber-transport aircraft and night bombers that was to arise from the WWI Vimy bomber. These manifested themselves as Victorias, Virginias and Valentias – the mainstay of the RAF heavy aircraft needs in the 1920s. The Virginia seen here after a particularly unfortunate touchdown in July 1925 is J7436, code letter N, a Mk.V of No. 58 Squadron based at Worthy Down where this mishap occurred. The machine was returned to Vickers for repair and it emerged that October as a Mk.IX and was the first Virginia to be converted for wheel brakes prior to flying with No 7 (Bombing) Squadron. It had also been planned to install automatic leading edge slots to the upper wings but instead these were fitted to another machine, J7720.

Bristol F.2B Fighters were known as 'Brisfits' to those that flew them. And even this diminutive was frequently shortened further to 'Biff'. No 4 Squadron RAF was a training flight based at Farnborough and had one Biff, J6713, which was used for hack duties. Sometime in the winter of 1926, again for reasons that are now lost, the aircraft just happened to stall and plunge through the roof of the Malplaquet Barracks, Aldershot. This picture was taken shortly afterwards and in the interim the badly-injured pilot had been rescued by the enthusiastic use of axes. His observer was unhurt as were two unfortunates who happened to be in the building at the time. The actual building survived until 1965, its location being just behind the present Rushmoor Fire Station.

Looking a little like an inspiration for a well-known modern statue in the north of England, this Fokker 7/3m was the first in use in America. It was operated by an outfit called the Philadelphia Rapid Transit Service on a special service inaugurated on July 16th 1926 in connection with that town's celebrations of the 150th anniversary of the Declaration of Independence flying three services a day between Philadelphia and Washington and charged a $25 return fare. On November 10th while landing at Hoover Field, Washington the aircraft got caught in a downdraught, both wing tips struck the ground and broke off and the aircraft overturned. All nine passengers were injured, two of them needing hospital treatment. It was a shame because by the time the service ended on November 30th, 3,700 passengers had been carried. US airline authority R E G Davies says that it was completed 'without incident'. This picture suggests otherwise!

The Felixstowe F.2A with its wide hull designed by John Cyril Porte was acclaimed as a successful and safe flying boat. Orders for 161 were placed in March 1918 but deliveries were delayed due to the extreme shortage of the Rolls-Royce Eagle engines. This unidentified example from the Royal Navy Air Service has clearly met with some unfortunate accident and has been beached broadside on. The starboard underside of the hull has been stove in at the nose and the fabric has been stripped from the underside of the tailplane. All this probably explains why the emergency mooring ropes have been attached to the wooden propeller-blades.

Flying boats have always been susceptible to weather and water conditions and many met with potentially serious problems. Alan Cobham had planned a round the world flight in a twin-engined Short Singapore, the first all-metal flying boat. With extra tankage it could cruise for eleven hours on 600 gallons of petrol and cover about 900 miles. However, even with that range it was not quite enough so he altered his plans, settling for a 23,000-mile survey flight around Africa to chart a possible route for Imperial Airways. Benefactor Sir Charles Wakefield, the oil-company magnate, put up £12,000 of his own money for the trip. On

November 20th 1927 the aircraft, registered G-EBUP and fitted with high-compression Rolls-Royce Condor IIIA engines each of 650 hp, set off from the River Medway. It was an arduous flight but having reached Malta on December 1st they were being towed by RAF launch across Marsa Scirocco Bay to Kalafrana when a huge wave hit broadside and snapped off the starboard wing float. As the aircraft tipped over, three crew – Hugh G Conway and a man named Green who were both Rolls-Royce engineers, and S R Bonnet, a Gaumont cameraman who was there to film the whole trip, ran up the wing to try to counterbalance the boat. Meanwhile the port float filled with water and also snapped off. It took two hundred men to drag the boat on its hull to safety, later sawing off the damaged port wing to clear a wall that impeded safe beaching. Shorts built a pair of new floats, a new wing and replacement elevators and had them out to Malta in two weeks. That was just one adventure, pictured here, and by the time the survey flight was finished there had been many other delays, mishaps and repairs – even a new engine. But Cobham returned to London triumphantly at the end of his epic flight.

Flying boats were curious structures in which all the superstructure, meaning wings and engines, was often attached to a suspended hull meaning that in a severe accident, it was not uncommon for the hull to be the sole remaining identifiable part. In the summer of 1928, several Southamptons were taking part in a training course in the Firth of Forth when one of them, flying too low, struck the mast of the tender *Adastral*. The impact was so severe that the wings and engines separated and the hull struck the water. This is all that was left in an accident which claimed the life of one crew member.

Many of the early attempts at flying Autogiros ended up with the aircraft lying on its side amidst a tangle of bent and broken rotor blades while a red (or white) faced pilot crawled shakily from his cockpit. Ground resonance was little understood and once the 'dancing' motion began there was little that could be done to stop it. The cause was not recognised in the early days although it was known that turning downwind or crosswind with the rotor spinning could initiate it during the preparations for take-off. Here in a unique if fuzzy snapshot we see 100 hp Avro Alpha engined Avro 620 Cierva/C.17 Mk.II G-AAGJ with its stub wings and upturned tips demonstrating the penultimate stages of ground resonance during the winter of 1928-29. The pilot was Arthur 'Dizzy' Rawson. He was unhurt and the Autogiro went on to become the sole example of the Hydrogiro flown from Southampton Water on April 25th 1930 but without markings. Afterwards it was dismantled and then, extraordinarily, it began a fresh existence as an Avro Avian Mk.IV registered G-ADEO on March 20th 1935. Finally it was impressed on January 17th 1940 as 2075M, the letter as a suffix indicating that it was allocated to a non-flying instructional airframe.

Amidst the more curious of the class of light aeroplanes that were styled 'homebuilt' in the decades between the wars, the curious Glenny & Henderson Gadfly was unusual in several respects. Built at York Road, Byfleet, Surrey, the business partners were A P Glenny who was a wealthy young man who had made his cash in cotton, and G L P Henderson, who was a pilot and instructor at Brooklands. The little Gadfly was a very lightly built machine – the fuselage longerons were five-eighths of an inch square – and not designed to be robust. Two aircraft were built. The second one was used to evaluate the special rotary ailerons devised by Gadfly designer Capt Kenneth Nobel Pearson. First flown in August 1929, shortly afterwards Glenny himself was flying this particular machine – G-AARJ – when the engine failed and he attempted a landing in a field next to the river at Wargrave on Thames. The undercarriage broke, removing a length of bottom longeron and causing the total break-up of the machine. Notice the uninterested glances of the youths passing by, also the girl in the cloche hat. The curious ovals at the wing extremities are the 'oyster' rotary ailerons.

This close-up of the cockpit area of G-AARJ reveals the flimsy construction and, centre right, how the engine has ended up facing the wing leading edge.

Pilot A P Glenny inspects the wreck of G-AARJ and no doubt ponders on how lucky he was to escape uninjured. Centre front of this picture is the cockpit windscreen and top-decking showing the fuel filler cap.

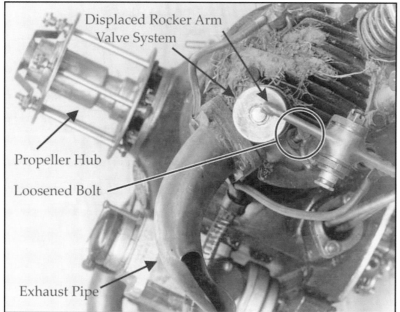

Displaced Rocker Arm
Valve System

Propeller Hub

Loosened Bolt

Exhaust Pipe

Why the Gadfly G-AARJ lost power and crashed is evident from this close-up picture of the 35 hp ABC Scorpion after its removal to the workshop. The exhaust valve rocker arm has worked loose in its bracket (the loose bolts are just visible under the rocker arm) so displacing the rocker from the valve. For all its shortcomings, the little Gadfly prototype managed to notch up a World attitude record of 3,021 m in the 200 kg class on May 16th 1929 piloted by Henderson. As for G-AARJ, it was rebuilt and sold to Canada where it became CF-AMG and lasted until destroyed by fire at Kitchener, Ontario, on August 25th 1931.

Many of the most historic aircraft are allowed to meet inglorious ends. Some, like Charles Ulm's great triple-motor'd monoplane, were simply abandoned in the open to rot away and be picked at by scavenging schoolboys. Others have been consciously committed to the aeronautical hereafter like the TSR-2 and Brabazon through stubborn ignorance at a high level. But Sir Charles Kingsford Smith's Gipsy II-powered long-range single-seat Avro Avian IVA was lost through pure carelessness. First registered on September 26th 1930, G-ABCF was a long-range model which Kingsford Smith named *Southern Cross Junior*. In it he lowered the England-Australia record to nine days and twenty-one hours that October. On January 7th 1931 a man from Sydney, Guy Lambton Menzies, made the first ever crossing of the Tasman Sea to New Zealand. Quite unannounced, he left Mascot New South Wales, at 12.40 am with 110 gallons of fuel. He covered the estimated 1,190 miles in twelve hours and fifteen minutes at an average speed of 97 mph, making landfall at Okarito, West Coast South Island. He now turned north along the coast to find a suitable landing place. With echoes of Allcock and Brown's epic Atlantic flight, he selected what he thought to be the solid bed of the Wangehu River near Herepo. Unfortunately it proved to be vegetated marshland and the Avian turned over with little damage. It was souvenir hunters that did the most damage to the aircraft which Menzies subsequently shipped back to Sydney aboard the *Aorangi* on February 10th 1931. Repaired, it was sold on to A E James and re-registered VH-UPT. On April 12th 1931 while being flown by L J Palmer with owner James as passenger, the aircraft attempted a loop but the port wing box folded back against the fuselage and a dual fatal crash followed. Cause? The wing-unfolding process had not been followed by pushing home the lower locking pin.

It was Saturday April 4th 1931 and the opening ceremony of the newly-laid-out Gatwick Aerodrome between the famous Gatwick Racecourse and the village of Lowfield Heath. In actual fact the first airfield licence had been issued on June 25th 1930 but the first months were for various reasons unsuccessful. Not until the Surrey Flying Club established new premises on Hunts Green Farm did Gatwick begin to look like an airfield proper. And then the Redwing Aircraft Company stepped in and made the place their headquarters. The opening day was a success with plenty of visiting aircraft when suddenly disaster struck. A de Havilland DH.60G Gipsy Moth G-ABHS (first registered January 6th 1931) was being started without chocks when without warning it started

off by itself, its erstwhile pilot being knocked to the ground. One-time famed amateur golfer Dale Bourne rushed forward to help but was caught by the propeller which broke his arm. Its path was eventually halted when it collided with another Moth which brought it to a spectacular and expensive halt. Both machines survived, G-ABHS eventually going to Poland in March 1933 as SP-ALK. Gatwick continued as a private aerodrome until the early post-war years when with the closure of the racecourse it expanded into London's second international airport.

N9811 Blackburn Dart was ordered for the Fleet Air Arm in August 1924. During exercises with HMS *Courageous* in the Mediterranean in the summer of 1929, the aircraft was being flown by Captain John M Fuller of the Royal Marines when he detected that the fuel tank was leaking badly and that he was out of petrol with no option other than to ditch next to the ship. Here we see the intrepid aviator perched on the highest surviving part of his ship (Americans tend to call aircraft 'ships' for linguistic simplicity but in this case perhaps the term is justifiable, even if only in the short-term). The flyer was rescued and went on to have a distinguished military career, retiring with the rank of colonel and eventually departing this world with dry feet in 1966.

On July 21st 1930 there was an unusual air crash which caused ripples of concern around the aeronautical world. In bad weather, single-engined Junkers F.13 registered G-AAZK broke up in mid-air at Meopham Green, Kent, falling in pieces into private grounds killing all six people on board. The dead included veteran pilot G L P Henderson and his second pilot C D Shearing, both from Croydon, but his passengers were in the 'gilt-edged' class – the Marquis of Dufferin and Ava, the Viscountess Ednam, Sir Edward Ward and Mrs Loeffler. The mystery was that the Junkers was a most successful tried and tested aircraft with an impeccable safety record. But examination of the remains shocked the experts for this was the first recorded incident of metal fatigue and this is why this dramatic accident has gone down in history. This picture shows how the aircraft has struck the ground upside down and, by the presence of the strands of a wire fence draped over the fuselage, turned on its nose from the inverted position.

Soon after it entered service with Imperial Airways at Croydon, the new giant HP.42 airliner Hannibal was on one of its usual European flights on the Croydon-Paris-Zürich service. It was August 8th 1931 and piloting G-AAGX was Captain Frederick Dismore. Without any warning a cowling fastener broke loose on one of the upper engines and damaged one blade of the port lower airscrew. This disintegrated and flying debris broke the two upper propellers. This in turn damaged the starboard lower airscrew. Without effective power, Dismore could not keep the airliner flying and so selected a small field at Tudeley near Tonbridge in Kent for a forced landing. All seemed well on the approach but at the last moment telephone wires were spotted and in attempting to avoid them the tail hit a concealed stump and was pulled off. Nobody was in any way hurt in this remarkable incident. This remarkable press photograph shows G-AAGX sitting in a tiny meadow having pulled up in a little over its own total length after breaking off its tail. It was found that the broken propeller blades had scythed through the fuselage between the two passenger cabins where, fortuitously, baggage compartment and galley were situated. Engineers armed with huge pairs of step-ladders descended on the machine and dismantled it prior to taking it by road the 35 miles to Croydon where it was repaired in Imperial Airways' workshops by Handley Page technicians.

In 1928 an order had been placed for 25 Hawker Horsley Mk.II aircraft powered by 665 hp Rolls-Royce Condor IIA engines. Fifth aircraft delivered was J8601 which was flying over Somerset on June 28th 1929 when, at 1,000 feet, the engine stopped through carburettor icing. Ironically the heatwave which gripped Britain that month did not prevent low-level icing conditions. In the ensuring forced landing the aircraft crashed and had to be rebuilt by Hawker. It returned to service and ended up with 100 Squadron marked '6'. In the autumn of 1931 it again crashed (pictured here) following a badly-judged crosswind landing which removed the undercarriage. This time it seems not to have flown again.

The palisades have saved more than a few naval pilots from an unexpected sock-wetting and this particular day was to save another. This particular Fairey IIIF, S1379, had started out in life as a Mk.III but had undergone conversion to 'F' standards at Hamble in 1930. Attached to HMS *Courageous*, this pilot was engaged in deck-landing practice in September 1930 when he swerved on landing and went over the side where, fortunately, he was ensnared in the protective netting while the gallant fleet of naval personnel who had the job of anticipating this sort of thing, dashed out to retrieve aeroplane and some of the pilot's self-esteem.

The decade from the mid 1920s until the mid 1930s produced a number of aviation entrepreneurs – people who became heroes of the time for their aeronautical achievements. Jean Batten, Amy Johnson, Sir Alan Cobham and Charles Lindbergh immediately spring to mind. But one who, surprisingly, is less well remembered today in this regard is Sir Francis Chichester (1901-72). He was both sailor and aviator, achieving fame with his Gipsy Moth yacht, its name chosen because he also flew the world in a Gipsy Moth. DH.60G Moth G-AAKK was owned by the Brooklands School of Flying and when Chichester wanted to fly to Darwin, Australia, they leased it to him. Bearing the name Madame Elijah, Chichester departed Croydon on December 20th 1929 and reached Darwin on January 25th 1930. He pressed on to Sydney which he reached on the

last day of the month. From there the Moth was taken by sea to New Zealand from whence Chichester planned to fly to Japan. The Moth was temporarily registered ZK-AKK and equipped with floats. On April 1st 1931 Chichester departed New Zealand en route for Japan via Lord Howe Island about 375 miles east of the Australian coast. Unfortunately the Moth capsized on landing at Lord Howe as seen in this snapshot. Repaired, he proceeded to Japan but the Moth was totally wrecked when he struck a sea wall when landing at Katsuura. There is a lot of confusion over the date of the second accident. Records give July 17th 1931 as the correct date; other sources July 14th and Chichester himself, writing much later, placed it at August 14th or 15th! This is known to historians as the mercurial mobility of uncertain facts…

The HP.42 airliner was still a new and marvellous aircraft when, on June 19th 1932, 37-year-old Captain Walter Rogers, later to be chief pilot for Imperial Airways, flew Heracles, first of the 'western' variants, into West London's Hanworth Aerodrome to give flights at the Royal Aeronautical Society's annual Garden Party. All went well until the 29,500 lb giant taxied across a covered culvert, the top of which promptly collapsed. The wheel sank deep into the hole allowing the wing-tip to land hard on the ground, so collapsing one of the diagonal inter-wing bracing struts. For the time being immovable, the engines were removed to lighten the aircraft for lifting out of the hole. The airframe was then pushed back against a protecting hedge and surrounded by a low security wooden paling fence while repairs were carried out on side. They took almost a month before, with a new lower outer wing and struts and the engines replaced, G-AAXC was able to return to Croydon. For the rest of its days Heracles was a record-breaker and, by July 23rd 1937 it had notched up a million flying miles on the Paris, Cologne and Zürich routes. A year later, on the seventh anniversary of its first scheduled flight, it had carried 95,000 passengers notching up more than a million and a quarter miles. Heracles was evacuated to Whitchurch at the outbreak of war along with sister machine Hanno. During a gale on March 19th 1940, they became partially airborne at their ground pickets and were blown into each other. So ended the days of not one but two of these monumental Handley Pages.

This picture, taken by *Flight's* photographer the following week, shows *Heracles* parked under the Hanworth hedge waiting a new port lower wing and outer rear interplane strut. Of interest here is the method of supporting the upper wing on ladder trestles. Secured to the top wing is one of the repositionable shear-leg hoists provided as onboard equipment to enable engine changes to be carried out on site. Here it is positioned immediately above the position of the removed port top motor. Visible on the actual photograph are mooring ropes tied to adjacent trees. The high security paling fence is also seen clearly here.

In the early 1930s there was quite a serious proposal put forward by reasonably intelligent people that London's Hyde Park should, at least in part, be turned into an aerodrome. Ordinary observers and readers of the daily papers must have thought that trials were under way when, on December 11th 1933 Bristol Bulldog K2189 puttered out of the skies and landed in the park, 'narrowly missing Marble Arch' as the newspaper stories told. It was, said Flying Officer Smith (seen standing disconsolately by the side of his plane) engine trouble that forced him to descend. Here we see the visitor surrounded by police and spectators as he awaits his further instructions. The following day it was, to the dismay of the hopefuls, dismantled and taken away by motor lorry.

A mystery, a tragedy and an unsolved mishap. It was December 20th 1933 at the Royal Air Force Station Abu Sueir in Egypt which was the home of No. 4 FTS and the training ground for many young Service pilots who were converted on to Armstrong Whitworth Atlas Mk.I biplanes. K1012 was delivered on July 21st 1930, one of a batch of 87 machines that had started in the 'J' series. The aircraft suddenly started up and, without permission, took off from the desert strip. It attempted to turn, stalled and spun in. The pilot and sole occupant turned out to be 560657 Leading Aircraftman John Joseph Francis McDermott who was killed on impact. At the subsequent inquest, nobody could explain why he had attempted to fly one of the King's aircraft with neither permission nor qualification. Was he just bored? With all those competent young pilots around, had he convinced himself that it must be just too easy to fly an Atlas? Or was he trying to fly home for Christmas? Nobody will ever know.

LAC McDermott had had several rides as passenger in Atlas aircraft. Denied Christmas home leave, it was thought that in a moment of desperation he reckoned that he would cast caution to the wind. The verdict was 'death by misadventure' but the real truth will never be known. The curious sight of what appears to be a yacht with sails in the background is a land-yacht on wheels: a popular sport and spare time activity was desert-sailing.

The DH.83 Fox Moth represented the height of luxury in 1932. It could carry four people in enclosed (if rather cramped) cabin comfort on a single 120 hp Gipsy Major engine. Built using some Tiger Moth parts, it was an instantaneous success and news that no less than the Prince of Wales was about to take possession of an example – G-ACDD finished in red, blue and rather a lot of chromium – boosted sales. In the end, though, His Royal Highness opted for the larger Dragon instead. But the Fox Moth was popular with the better class of joy-riding and air taxi operator. Registered on March 30th 1933, G-ACEA was used by Renfrew-based Scottish Motor Traction Co Ltd. A year later the aircraft attempted a forced landing in a field of knee-high potatoes. This was sufficient to flip it over rather gently – the rudder never even touched the ground. However, both forward interplane struts were damaged – that on the starboard side was temporarily replaced with a wooden fence-post presumably to avoid further damage while righting the machine. Somebody here has thrown a rope around the tail. Repaired and restored, it went to the Sussex & Wilmington Aero Club in March 1936, was sold to the Sandown & Shanklin Flying Club at Lea in that July, was transferred with the renaming of the club as the Isle of Wight Flying Club in July 1939 and was impressed in June 1940 as AW 140. Soon it was of no further value and so was scrapped in April 1944.

It is August 1934 and this three-month old DH.60GIII Moth Major of the Household Brigade Flying Club has made unfortunate landfall in a field near Burghfield Bridge in Berkshire. Contact with a tree has collapsed the port centre-section pylon, broken the undercarriage (the port wheel is missing), halved the propeller and performed rather rough surgery on the lower port wing. The aircraft, G-ACPI, was later dismantled and carted back to its base at Heston for repair. It went on to fly for many a further year being sold abroad in May, 1940.

The prototype Armstrong Whitworth AW.15 Atalanta for Imperial Airways first flew in August 1932 but that October suffered a serious accident in a forced landing. Rebuilt, it became VT-AEF for Indian Trans-Continental Airways and was named *Arethusa*. In 1934, during a visit by the Duke of Northumberland, the aircraft became bogged down at Kuala Lumpur. On this occasion the command 'All out and push!' proved insufficient.

One of *Arethusa's* wheels well and truly stuck in the soft ground at Kuala Lumpur. The Atalanta was unusual in having its main undercarriage attached entirely to the fuselage as can be seen in this snapshot. Note also the vestigial wheel-spats provided to keep most of the mud thrown up by the wheels off the wing underside and the windows. The full-sized spatted fairings fitted to the prototype were abandoned following concerns over the effects of mud building up inside them, freezing at altitude and then grasping the wheel solid on landing.

S1662 was one of a batch of 26 Blackburn Ripon II torpedo-bombers all of which were converted to Baffins with 565 hp Bristol Pegasus IM3 radials. Some 29 examples were built as Baffins while 68 Ripons were upgraded. Deliveries started early in 1934 and were completed in June 1935. 'Landing on' was and still today is a tricky task. Here S1662 of 810 Squadron makes a bit of a pig's ear of the job on HMS *Courageous* in the summer of 1934.

All too frequent causes of mishaps, especially at training aerodromes, were simply not seeing the other aircraft. When this happened in flight, the outcome was more usually fatal as aircraft flying into each other tend to form an unsurvivable event. When it happens on the ground and barring those not uncommon occasions when somebody has been struck by a fast-turning propeller, the outcome is more usually survivable and the accompanying wreck more amusing than horrific. On October 29th 1934, two Avro Tutors of No 5 FTS Seaford had an airfield assignation. K3251 had just landed and was taxiing in when K3263, landed on its tail. The latter was restored and carried on flying for another four years but the victim was too badly damaged to escape being no more than 'reduced to produce'. Sadly the rear cockpit occupant was fatally injured.

J9596 was a Westland Wapiti Mk.IIA which went to No.602 City of Glasgow Squadron based at Renfrew. That autumn this aircraft was involved in a curious mishap portrayed in this picture. In attempting a forced landing following losing his bearings, the pilot struck the top of an earth bank on finals which thrust him back into the air. At full power the machine stalled, port lower wing and nose striking the ground. The picture shows the unlikely outcome: right landing gear broken, left wheel with burst tyre and half embedded in the ground, engine thrust backwards and wooden propeller splintered due to high revs. It was, even more strangely, deemed beyond economic repair and was scrapped. The associated damage to the front fuselage must have been worse than it appeared.

The well-proportioned Fairey Seal was a development of the very successful Fairey IIIF and the Gordon biplane. It could be used as a normal landplane with the option of a floatplane conversion. Built to carry a 500 lbs bomb load and defended by one fixed Vickers gun and a movable Lewis, the three-man biplane was well-respected and the 91 examples built enjoyed a long and productive life. Pictured here is K3537, code 729, which was assigned to 821 Squadron engaged in fleet spotter reconnaissance. It was delivered to Gosport on June 15th 1933 and served on HMS *Courageous*. In September 1934, however, it flew into high ground in bad visibility and was wrecked.

This view of Fairey Seal K3537 gives a good indication that the machine struck at high speed for the metal propeller has both blades bent back around the nose, the engine mounting has fractured and the undercarriage has been forced up through the lower wing mainspars.

The tale of de Havilland DH.84 Dragon I G-ACCR is not a happy one as the following pictures testify. Registered on April 3rd 1933 it was first owned by W A Rollason at Croydon before going to Barnstaple & North Devon Air Services that October. In December the following year it came back to Croydon in charge of The Hon Mrs Victor Bruce's company, Commercial Air Hire Ltd. Just two months later, on February 27th 1935 while engaged on its Croydon-Paris newspaper run, it flew into thick fog and force-landed in a muddy field at Sarcelles in the Val d'Oise some 10 miles north of the centre of Paris and a mere three and a half miles short of Le Bourget Airport. This was the result. On this occasion matters were quickly put right and the flight completed after a delay of just a few hours.

After its nose-stand in France, Dragon G-ACCR was destined only to last another eleven months. The faithful old DH.84 did, though, go out in style and, happily, without seriously hurting anybody. Pilot Jackson flew a consignment of gold bullion valued at £80,000 to Paris on the evening of January 21st 1936, leaving Le Bourget for the return flight at 23.15 hrs. On board with him were both Commercial Air Hire Ltd's wireless telegraphy operators, Messrs Burgess and Philpott. The weather report was good with a cloudless and moonless sky. At 00.20 hrs he crossed the coast at Le Tréport on course for Bexhill flying at 1,850 feet. An unexpected shower of hail was prelude to a storm. The propellers began to display halos of purple light and a purple glow spread along the leading edge of the upper wing. There was a flash inside the aircraft and a loud bang – and the W/T went out. Jackson then noticed the compass was not working and he flew two circuits to no avail – the card appeared to be immovably stuck. He steered for the one visible beacon light – Le Tréport – but despite full throttle both engines gradually lost power and so aware of the high chalk cliffs and shoreline rocks in the area he put down in the sea using the trailing wireless aerial as a height indicator. The aircraft landed tail first and settled in about eight feet of water. After exiting through the cockpit roof escape hatch and sitting on the wing in the dark they decided to swim for it. They were about a mile and a half the Ault side of Dieppe and then had the difficult task of finding help. By now it was after two in the morning and those cottages upon whose doors they knocked were understandably unhelpful. Eventually a small hotel was found. The next morning they went back to the Dragon which by now had been shorn of its rear fuselage and tail. In an effort to save the engines they dragged the remains ashore parking them above the high water mark of the beach against the vertical cliff face. Here rescuers, helpers and hangers-on pose for posterity with the tattered remains of a Dragon that was the victim of static electricity.

One of Commercial Air Hire Ltd's other Dragons suffered a tragic end for it proved unnecessarily profligate in its fatalities which included a young engaged couple. This was G-ACAP, one of Hillman's Airways Ltd's original machines first registered on February 9th 1933. Hillman's sold it to CAH in February 1936. Its end would come just a month later when, on the night of March 26th and while engaged in searchlight manoeuvres for the Territorial Army under an Army Co-operation contract, it crashed and burned at Stonycross in the New Forest. The twin-engined aircraft had been assigned to making circuits in the Southampton area between 6,000 feet and 8,000 feet. Why it crashed remains a mystery to this day although at 20.07 hrs the pilot, Francis Joseph Birmingham, sent a wireless message saying he was at 9,000 feet and had noticed ice formation. The next thing was that the machine hit the ground at the foot of one of the highest points in Hampshire. Both engines were found to have been running at more or less full power and the speed of impact was estimated to have been about 150 mph. With a maximum speed of around 128 mph, this would suggest the aircraft was in a steep dive. Pilot and wireless operator Robert Frank Burgess were, of course, killed. But it was found that there were also three 'unauthorised' passengers on board the aircraft – people which the company had allowed to go along 'for the ride. These were the brother of the pilot, Mr R Rendon Birmingham, Norman Tyrell Burton and 17-year-old Daisy Marsh who had just become engaged to W/T operator Burgess. The inquest took place at Lyndhurst on March 30th at which a verdict of 'Death from Misadventure' was recorded. It left many questions unanswered. The only 'fact' that was 'established' was that the aircraft did not seem to have experienced any in-flight failures. Although a cold and almost clear-sky'd night, it seems unlikely that icing would have been the sole cause of loss of control resulting in a crash. Were the passengers in any way responsible? Nobody will ever know.

It was Mrs Bruce's main company, Air Dispatch Ltd, which suffered a strange accident on the night of January 22nd 1937. What was odd about this one is that despite crashing in what would normally be thought of as a densely populated area, it took two days to find the wreckage! G-ADBZ was an almost new Airspeed Envoy I first registered on April 6th 1935. It had seen service with North Eastern Airways Ltd where it was named *Swaledale*. In 1936 it was leased to Air Dispatch for the daily Croydon-Paris newspaper run. It left Croydon at 06.00 hrs piloted by 39-year-old G S Jones-Evans with James Walker as wireless operator. They disappeared and, having received no radio communication from them back at Croydon, when they were reported overdue at Le Bourget a massive air and sea search began. At midnight the following day, the wreckage was found strewn in a wood near Titsey Hill corner, a mere few miles from Croydon. The crew was dead, the aircraft had disintegrated and its cargo scattered throughout the ancient wood. Jones-Evans, an RFC/RAF pilot in the First War, had only joined the company two weeks earlier.

A police constable picks over the cargo of undelivered newspapers in the wood at Titsey Hill.

This De Havilland DH.60G, G-AAJZ, was first registered on July 19th 1929 and owned by The Hon. Mrs A P Westenra. On Friday January 24th 1936, it was being flown by David H Jorge of Croydon when he was caught over north London in a bank of fog. Disorientated, he emerged from the murk at a height he estimated as being eighty feet leaving him no room to avoid making a crash-landing into unoccupied kennels at the Ministry of Agriculture's quarantine station in Kingsdale Hill, Stanmore, Middlesex. This picture, taken from the pages of the following day's *Daily Express*, show the tiny space into which the Moth was packed. The aircraft was repaired and was operated by the Redhill Flying Club until 1940. It survived to be impressed on January 25th 1941 as DG586 but was unceremoniously scrapped in June 1945.

The Westland Wapiti IIA was powered by a 550 hp Bristol Jupiter VIII radial engine and this example, J9392, entered service in 1931 with No 15 (Reserve) Squadron at Martlesham Heath. In July 1936 it was engaged in combined operations at Shoeburyness when it failed to pull out of a dive and struck the ground at high speed, breaking the fuselage into three pieces and collapsing the wings. It was beyond repair.

Avro Cadet II G-AENL, first registered on September 16th 1936, was on a training flight from Hamble on April 8th 1937 when the 135 hp Armstrong Siddeley Genet Major I engine faltered and the student pilot was faced with his first ever attempt at a forced landing. He did it in style, landing upside down in a Hamble back garden. It is related that the pilot scrambled out of the inverted biplane and apologised profusely to the occupier of the house for the damage he had caused. The Cadet was repaired and flew on to be impressed on August 28th 1941 as one of the unusual 'M-suffix' series as 2951M and passed to No 580 Air Training Corps Squadron at Dauntsey's School, Wiltshire.

One of the most memorable airliner accidents of the 1930s happened just outside Croydon Airport on the morning of December 9th 1936. A DC-2, PH-AKL, of the Dutch airline KLM was taking off in fog following Croydon's famous white line painted on the ground to provide a directional reference in just such conditions. The pilot made two take-off attempts but on each occasion lost sight of the line and turned back. On the third occasion he again veered but took the decision to continue. Swinging ever away from the proper line the big twin took off in a wide left turn but struck the roof of a house on the airfield side of Hillcrest Road, cartwheeled over the street and struck the front of No 25 which, fortunately, was empty and for sale or rent at the time. A total of fourteen people died in the ensuing inferno, among them the man who invented the Autogiro, Juan de la Cierva, and a former Swedish Prime Minister, Admiral Arvid Lindman. Only three survived – a German passenger, the wireless operator and the stewardess who was flung out as the machine crossed the road. An irony is that the stewardess was a long-term Nazi collaborator who was tried after the end of the war and is believed to have paid with her life. The photograph was taken the next morning after the fire had been extinguished and that killer fog dispersed.

Hawker's Audax was a development of the Hart and was used extensively for training. All had chequered histories and this particular machine, K4397, was no exception. Delivered new to No 6 Flying Training School in October 1934, it subsequently had a contretemps with the wind direction during landing which resulted in the landing gear being wiped off. It was rebuilt after this October 1936 mishap but met its end at 03.00 hrs on June 18th 1937 when its pilot, engaged in night flying practice, got lost and attempted a forced landing at Maiden Bradley, six miles south-south-west of Warminster in Wiltshire. The pilot escaped with serious injuries.

This Hawker Audax K3069 served with 26 Squadron in 1933 and gave good service until June 25th 1937 when it undershot on landing at Catterick, ran into long grass and overturned. Pilot J Curtiss was unhurt but the aircraft was struck off charge soon afterwards.

Aeroplanes did seem to fall out of the sky more often in the past than they do today. Perhaps that's something we should all be thankful for, although modern aircraft tend to do much more damage when they descend unintentionally or unadvisedly. It was just before lunch on Friday June 11th 1937 when the people of Yate near Bristol acquired a fresh if temporary visitor attraction. Tiger Moth G-ACZY, first registered on November 12th 1934, was operated by Filton Flying School and on this occasion was being flown by Reginald Tomkins of Maestag Glamorgan. Nobody seems to know quite what happened, least of all the chap who was flying it, but it came down unexpectedly narrowly missing (in the words of the *Daily Mirror*) 'two walls, a fence and a lamp-post'. Nobody was hurt except the pilot who broke his leg. The Moth was retrieved, repaired and sold to India in February 1941 where it became VT-ANZ.

Designed for the 1937 King's Cup Race by students of the de Havilland Technical College at Hatfield, the TK.4 was a truly remarkable machine. With a span of nineteen feet eight inches and a length of fifteen and a half feet, the design speed was more than 200 mph driven by the power of a 140 hp Gipsy Major II engine. More unusual was the fact that, despite its tiny size and slender high performance wing, it had a fully-retractable undercarriage and split trailing-edge flaps. The wing-section was symmetrical and so shallow in chord depth that four solid spars were required. Retractable flush-fitting leading edge slots each three feet in length were provided on each wing. Wide use of balsa wood for fairings plus the use of a magnesium alloy called Elektron for the rear fuselage cockpit-to-fin superstructure contributed to an empty weight of just 928 lbs. The use of a moulded Perspex windscreen was, at the time, revolutionary and it also made history for being the first British aircraft of any type to have its engine cowlings secured by the new flush-fitting American-made Dzus fasteners. The first flight was on July 30th 1937 by DH test pilot Robert John Waight. The machine then went to Martlesham Heath for C of A trials. There it was described as handling very well up to its maximum speed of 235 mph but the stalling speed, flaps up, was very high at 95 mph. On September 1st the C of A was granted and the machine entered for the King's Cup Race due on September 11th. In the actual race, although handicapped to a ninth-place finish, it achieved an average of 234 mph on one leg. It was then decided to go for two International Class records – fastest speed over 100km and then the 1,000km. Bob Waight took off on October 1st for the attempt. Possibly due to a high speed stall, the aeroplane suddenly dived into the ground and took 28-year-old Bob Waight to an instant death. The effect on the morale at the Technical College was devastating while de Havilland had lost an ace pilot.

Shocked and stunned staff and students survey the end of the fastest racing aircraft the DH Technical College had ever designed and built following the crash just outside Hatfield Aerodrome on October 1st 1937.

One of a batch built by Armstrong Whitworth at Whitley Abbey between December 1934 and April 1935, Hawker Hart K4483 saw service in the Middle East where, on November 1st 1937 it suffered in-flight engine failure necessitating a forced landing on the Jerusalem to Beersheba road. As this picture shows, the undercarriage collapsed and the aircraft had to be dismantled for recovery by road. It went on to fly for some further years before being transferred to the Egyptian Air Force on March 16th 1939.

Identifying the Hawker Hart biplane family can be rather confusing for it has so many similar-looking variants. This, though, is a Hardy which was developed from the Audax and intended for general purpose duties. It was introduced in September of 1934 and of the 47 built the first 21 had Rolls-Royce Kestrel IB engines of 530 hp. The balance, including K4312 seen here, were powered by the 585 hp Kestrel X. The type saw service in Iraq and Palestine (Ramleh). This particular example was delivered on May 31st 1935 and in the following January was at Hinaidi as reserve for No 10 Squadron. It then went to Aboukir in April of 1938 for service with No 6 Squadron. Marked with the squadron code letters ZD-O, it suffered the fate of a number of these high-powered, high-thrust-line biplanes in that it swung on take-off at Haifa on October 11th 1938 and the pilot over-corrected. At the best of times a 'twitchy' type to handle on the ground, this Hardy burst its port type, stood on its port wing tip and then came to rest as seen here. Repaired on site, it served another year before being struck off charge on November 30th 1939. A sister machine, K4315 also with the same squadron, flew the last Hardy operational mission as late as May 9th 1941.

Landing on flooded tarmac at Haifa in November 1938 proved more than this Fairey Gordon of No. 6 Squadron could cope with. Pilot F/O Ballam and his passenger, Aircraftman O'Connor escaped unhurt.

The great era of Imperial Airways' flying boat services marked a pinnacle of passenger excellence in the late 1930s yet was also one of the least cost-effective for the airline. The infrastructure for operating flying boat services was complex and expensive, labour-intensive and unreliable: there was always the overlay of weather and sea conditions that would scupper the smooth running of services and even the transit of passengers and luggage to and from the moored boat. Refuelling and servicing necessitated special equipment and techniques. Above all, flying boats were incredibly vulnerable to water-borne problems and unserviceability through striking flotsam was an ever-present hazard. Short Brothers at Rochester in Kent built a total of nine S.30 boats, larger versions of the S.23 Empire machines. G-AFCZ was named *Australia* and gained her C of A on April 6th 1939 and went into service with Imperial immediately. Its operation suffered a setback when, on August 9th 1939 – less than a month before the outbreak of war – it was severely damaged during take-off at Basra, the under nose and hull severely stove in breaking the keel and both chines. Here we see it drawn up out of the water onto the hard at Basra Airport using beaching gear. Dismantled on site and shipped back to Rochester it was quickly repaired and re-named Clare before re-entering service in October 1939. This one was eventually lost at sea off West Africa on September 24th 1942.

Some aircraft seem to be dogged by misfortune and few can have led such a life of despair as Vickers Valentia K4635 which was delivered to Worth Down on July 12th 1937 where it was fitted with Bristol Pegasus IIM3 engines. On the 29th of that month it left for India arriving at the Drigh Road aircraft depot on August 12th. Here it joined the base training flight on September 2nd and was allocated the code letter C. On February 8th 1936 while landing at Fatchgarh it ran into a gunnery target on landing and sustained some damage which was repaired on site. On July 9th 1937 it was taking off from Kohat when it struck a wandering ox and an undercarriage leg collapsed. After repairs the unit was absorbed into No 31 Squadron on April 1st 1939. The last ever flight of K4635 took place on August 27th 1939. A fuel vapour lock caused both engines to fail on take-off at Risalpur whereupon the aircraft dropped onto surrounding buildings. This time the damage was deemed too great to be worth fixing. The picture shows the inevitable crowd of watchers as the crew, shaken but safe, scramble out.

This, G-ACBG, is one of the few DH.82 Tiger Moths that were built. First registered on December 20th 1932 it gave good service until May 20th 1939 when it had the misfortune to spin in at Filton Junction. The man with the pork pie hat at the sharp end looks like an insurance assessor although it is not hard to see that this Tiger has met its match and, as the Americans would say, 'been totalled'. Very soon after this machine was built, the spinning characteristics were tamed by the introduction of anti-spin strakes and the creation of the DH.82a version.

Short Singapore Mk.III K8566, code letter B and nicknamed 'Bitsy', was first used by 210 Squadron in January 1937, transferring to 240 Squadron in November 1938. Used for training, the Squadron's sole Singapore was already an obsolete type but was thought adequate to give pilots experience in handling aircraft on water. On July 15th 1939 she met her end in what was actually a rare type of accident – a collision with a ship. The paddle steamer *Gracie Fields*, 393 gross tonnage, was launched in 1936 and plied the Southampton to Cowes route for Red Funnel Steamers, then known as the 'Original Isle of Wight ferry operator'. K8566 was taking off on a training flight when she developed an uncontrollable swing – and as she became airborne she struck the ship's mast with her starboard wings. The port bow of the *Gracie Fields* was damaged as the mast snapped and fell into the sea, the wings broke off the

flying boat outboard of the engines, the aircraft swung round and hit the water sideways, somehow coming to rest on an even keel with her intact port wings now sitting across the ship's bow. In all this mayhem nobody was hurt and in this picture, taken from the wheelhouse of the damaged ship, the flying boat crew is seen awaiting the rescue launch. The flying boat was deemed beyond economic repair and struck off charge, the *Gracie Fields* was repaired but was lost in 1940. Requisitioned for minesweeping, after just one successful trip she was hit by a bomb and badly damaged. Her crew were taken off by HMS *Pangbourne* which then attempted to tow the ship to safety. However, her rudder was jammed and she was taking on water, and she finally went to the bottom on May 30th.

Nicknamed 'Stringbag', the much-loved Fairey Swordfish was a formidable weapon of the Royal Navy. Like the Fairey IIIF series that it replaced, it was a powerful and productive workhorse built for the rough and tumble of the sea-travelling aircraft carrier. Judging the pitching of the deck in a rough sea was an art for not every manoeuvre took place in calm waters when all you had to worry about was the hook and which wire you were likely to miss. Built in December of 1937, L2824 was allocated to 810 Squadron on the Ark Royal in which deployment she took the squadron identity letters of A2A. In December 1939 an unintentionally hard landing neatly folded the hitherto fixed undercarriage and, as the deck came up, the engine broke free of its mount, spilling petrol which immediately ignited. In this snapshot taken as the flames took hold, the three-man crew is vacating the aircraft with an understandable degree of alacrity.

Any landing outside an aerodrome attracts crowds. And any mishap is the excuse for a public gathering. When only hardware and pride are shattered, the atmosphere can become quite jolly as it did when Avro Anson Mk.I K67226 of No.3 OTU skidded on rain-sodden grass at Hooton Park on October 17th 1941. The pilot's desperate but ultimately failed attempt to slew the aircraft around before the fence arrived drew an admiring crowd. Interesting to note is the number of women joining in the fun.

The Hawker Hart light bomber was the harbinger of a whole dynasty of similar or derivative biplanes that formed the Royal Air Force's equipment during the 1930s. K3921 was delivered in October 1934 and went out to India to serve with No 11 Squadron at Drigh Road aircraft depot. Later, on March 17th 1942 and while with No 1 Service Flying Training School, it overshot on landing at Ambala and struck a concrete pillar which damaged the undercarriage and, more to the point, cropped several useful feet off the wooden propeller. In the ensuing forced landing the undercarriage collapsed and the machine slithered to a halt on belly and left lower wing. Here the aircraft is seen in the company of the mandatory fire extinguisher in otherwise delightful settings.

Another view of Hawker Hart K3921. The aircraft was subsequently repaired and flew for another two years before being struck off charge in July 1944.

Many aircraft possess 'blind spots'. The majority of them are found seated in the pilot's cockpit! The Avro Anson was particularly prone to restricted downward vision for which the skilled pilot made allowances. Because the aircraft was used extensively for flying training, though, it was frequently entrusted to novice flyers for whom airspace seemed not just infinite but possessed of the spirit of the jealous guard. For this reason there are at least three instances where one aircraft has successfully landed on top of another and got away with it. Here is the sort of tangle that ensues when a pair of Mk I Ansons get frisky. Note the helmeted cowlings and the smooth cylinder baffles. That they are training aircraft is seen by the presence of the pair of landing lights in the leading edges of the port wings. This incident may have been one of the numerous mishaps at No 18 Service Flying Training School at Cranbourne in Southern Rhodesia during the war years. Somebody probably cried 'Chuck a bucket of water over 'em!'

No accident is ever planned – unless it is one of those expensive set-ups for the film industry. However, some activities that pilots practice are more risky than others. Take banner-towing (aerial advertising) for example. There had been several mishaps with this activity across the inter-war years but when it restarted after 1946 operators thought they had ironed out all the bugs. The technique was simple enough. A mesh of ribbons was used on which to clip canvas letters up to a given maximum. The 'message' would then be laid out on the airfield so that the

banner extended down-wind with the first letter at the front. From the end of the banner, a strong slender nylon rope was arranged in a long U-shaped loop at the end of which would be the towing aircraft. This faced into wind, took off and as it flew along parallel to the banner, it peeled the rope off the ground and, finally, the message itself would be peeled back and into the air. This was done to avoid any risk of the canvas letters catching on anything on the ground. On June 4th 1947 Taylorcraft Auster 5 (ex-TW478) was preparing to banner-tow at Denham. The normal process as described was followed but something went very wrong long before the banner was peeled. The Auster was airborne as the nylon rope loop was lifted off the ground but suddenly it snagged on a stout tuft of grass. The rope caught firm and began to stretch. The aircraft, by now at about 80 feet, began to slow as the rope tugged. At full throttle, the Auster stalled on the end of the cord and fell pancake-flat to the grass below. The Auster received such severe damage that it never flew again. Worse was the fact that the pilot, a flying instructor, went through his seat and broke his spine. Although recovered, he did not fly again.

Some accidents are memorable for various reasons but – and this is important – all accidents are unique events for no two are ever alike. Similar, possibly, but never *exactly* the same! Really memorable accidents are few and far between but one that certainly holds out fresh in my own memory is that of the Douglas DC-3 Dakota in Ruislip. At that time, the majority of commercial air traffic and its scheduled services had shifted from Croydon and Heston to Northolt while the new site at Heathrow was being built. Northolt was the headquarters of BEA and the largest of the secondary operators, Railway Air Services. Two weeks before Christmas 1946 there began in earnest one of the coldest and hardest winters we had experienced for many years. Low temperatures and heavy snow made life tough at a time when it was mostly a few public buildings that had central heating and everybody else still had open coal fires or gas-fires. On December 19th, Dakota G-AGZA (ex-KG420) was being prepared for take-off on the scheduled service to Glasgow. It would have a crew of four and just one passenger, Mr John Livingstone, a one-time Imperial Airways engineer. The aircraft took off but it was clear to everybody from the air traffic controller to the sole passenger that the aircraft could not climb. Fighting for non-existent altitude it dragged through telephone wires on the GWR's London-Birmingham railway line just outside South Ruislip London Transport station, cleared sheds in wasteland allotments, crossed Victoria Road and then, flying parallel to Angus Drive, the port wing struck the first of a number of rooftops in a newly-built and only partially-occupied housing development. The penultimate one was a heavy impact that caused the aircraft to veer 90 degrees, cross the road and finally came to rest fairly and squarely in the roof of a pair of semi-detached houses – numbers 44 and 46.

The take-off in a howling blizzard had followed a lengthy process of de-icing the wings. Then the aircraft taxied out to the runway threshold but was held some minutes for incoming traffic. During that crucial time the temperature dropped three degrees and fresh snow froze onto the wing surfaces. Following an abnormally long take-off run, both John Livingstone and stewardess Robina Christie knew that the flight was doomed. A quick-thinking tower controller saw the sluggish take-off and had already thumped the crash-bell before the aircraft went through the railway-line 'phone wires. Passenger and stewardess instinctively braced themselves for impact. As the aircraft came to a halt, both the pilot W J Johnson and his co-pilot and flight engineer were unhurt. Miraculously there were no other injuries. A four-month old boy, David Sigmund, was asleep in the bedroom of No 44 but he, too, escaped, sleeping soundly through a shower of ceiling plaster. No 46, newly furnished, was empty at the time. Despite leaking huge quantities of petrol from its full tanks, there was no fire.

Because the fuselage's main passenger door was over the edge of the roof, the four-strong crew plus their passenger got out of the aircraft via the over-wing emergency exit into the attic of No 46, opened the roof hatch and climbed down to the upstairs landing, walked down the stairs and let themselves out of the front door. They had crashed less than a mile from the end of Northolt's runway. In removing the aircraft from its perch, more damage was done to the house which was about to become the first home of a newly-married couple. It took six months to restore the building. It was ten years before oil stains ceased to keep appearing on ceilings and showing through the paintwork of Mr & Mrs Levene's restored home. Captain Johnson survived with the nickname 'Rooftop' and to this day there's a house in Angus Drive with the curious name *Dakota's Rest*.

While trying out a friend's brand new camera, I photographed Auster J/1 Autocrat G-AGXC at Denham on January 21st 1946. As we watched, the aircraft approached too high to land over the road whereupon the pilot pulled up the nose into a steep starboard turn, put up the flaps – and then opened the throttle. The sequence was as described. The poor Auster did what it could but airspeed eluded it as it stalled, completed one turn of a spin from 100 feet and went straight into the trees. We were first on the scene to help out two shocked and shaken fliers who immediately walked the length of the wing underside, crunching what was left of ribs and fabric as they went. Knowing we had a good shot of the aircraft entering the trees, we took the film straight up to Fleet Street, sold it and the story to *The Sunday Pictorial* and earned ourselves ten guineas!

Recipes for disaster are almost as numerous as disasters themselves but the mixture of youth, the summertime rising of the sap and pretty girls has a history of being a rather strong cocktail. When you add in a new aeroplane that's where the danger emerges. This is a picture taken on the beach at Shanklin on the Isle of Wight of a two-month old Auster Autocrat G-AJRD after it had been dragged up onto the sand by local boatmen. A young company director from Cowes whose pilot's licence was the same age as his aeroplane, took two young ladies for a joy-ride. One was his business partner and the other a local hotel employee. They circled low over a speedboat full of holidaymakers sailing just East of Shanklin pier and then pulled up steeply to about 150 feet at which point gravity took command. The silver and red Auster hit the water a few hundred yards off the crowded beach. As anybody who has misjudged a pool-dive and belly-flopped onto water will tell you, water is extremely hard. The aeroplane was wrecked. Help was on hand immediately and within moments boatmen and holidaymakers had quickly pulled the wreck up onto the foreshore. Tragically all had been killed on impact. It was Friday, August 29th 1947.

Immediately after the war, almost every British airliner in the skies was a Dakota. This made for standardisation of parts and services, but it also meant that every accident involved a Dakota. When newspapers started writing headlines such as 'Another Dakota crashes' the type gained a poor reputation amidst those for whom logical thinking was a foreign subject. By 1947 the newly-designed 'Wellington Transport Aircraft' (better known as the Vickers Viking) was in service and so this began to share the mishap headlines. Certainly there were a lot of mishaps in these early post-war years and some of these were due to attempting to fly in weather for which at that time insufficient navigational aids were available. An instance of this concerned Viking G-AHPK which joined the British European Airways fleet on April 14th 1947 and took the name *Veracity*. It left Glasgow for London (Northolt) on the evening of January 6th 1948. In pouring rain, poor visibility and distressingly too low on its approach, the all-silver airliner clipped the top of an elm tree at Ruislip Lido before crashing into woodland just one and a quarter miles short of the BEA base aerodrome of Northolt. The pilot lost his life, the first officer and radio officer escaped with injuries and six of the passengers were taken to Hillingdon Hospital for minor injury treatment. The picture shows one of those trivial quirks of fate that newspapers thrive on – the survival of a cabinet of wine-glasses, all unbroken.

The Gloster Meteor T.7 was the RAF's first jet trainer when it entered service in December 1948. It differed from the fighter version by having the front fuselage extended by 30 inches to make room for the second cockpit. In doing so it also dispensed with the huge lead ballast weight that all the fighters had fitted to the nosewheel structure. Unarmed, the tandem T.7 had full dual control and the engines were Rolls-Royce Derwent Mk.V (some later examples had Derwent Mk. VIII engines). Based at RAF Leuchars in Fife was 222 Squadron which, along with 43 Squadron, both operated Meteor T.8 fighters. Each squadron also had a T.7 for training and refresher use. That on the strength of 'Treble-Two' was VZ633 coded ZD-Z. During an exercise in the summer of 1949 a flame-out at low altitude over the coastal plain left no alternative but a 'wheels-up' in a field of freshly-baled hay. Here's the result – surprisingly little damage after a 120 mph touchdown!

The Auster Flying Club's annual display was staged at Rearsby Aerodrome in Leicestershire on July 10th 1949. One of the star turns was a spirited demonstration of the new Cierva Skeeter helicopter flown by Alan Marsh. The only thing to mar an otherwise fine day was the loss of G S Baker's Cierva C.30A G-AIOC. All Autogiro accidents tended to be spectacular but this one was especially so and the resulting damage judged irreparable. The shattered rotor curving upwards shows the rib attachments as closely-spaced projections. This example had been built for the RAF as an Avro Rota K4239 delivered to A & AEE on March 23rd 1935 seeing duty in radar calibration work with 26 Squadron and, later, 529 Squadron before being one of four sold off in the summer of 1946. Its first post-war owner was Basil H Arkell with whom I flew in this machine in 1947.

Auster J-5B Autocar G-AJYK was first registered on April 1st 1950 and was destroyed nine months later on September 18th in this crash four miles north of Leicester and next to the railway line. This high speed impact resulted from a spin that became a spiral dive and was pictured shortly afterwards by Auster's test pilot Ranold Porteous. It was not rebuilt.

Another snapshot from the camera of Auster's test pilot Ranold Porteous shows the aftermath of a mid-air collision between G-AHCJ and G-AIJY. The former appears to have come off the worse if only because its wheels are pointing upwards, while the latter merely looks forlorn. This incident took place at Speeton on September 9th 1948.

Some aircraft are a bit like cats in that, allegedly, they have more than one life. Certainly the story of Lockheed Constellation NC90606 is a candidate for rumours of reincarnation. Registered G-AHEN on April 6th 1946 and named *Baltimore*, this elegant American copy of de Havilland's pre-war Albatross entered service with British Overseas Airways Corporation and was used on the transatlantic service. The route in those days normally took in Shannon and Gander as refuelling stops. On a crew training flight on January 8th 1951, a heavy blizzard created a white-out and the aircraft missed its landing direction, coming to rest atop a conveniently small airport building. Extensively damaged at the sharp end, the aircraft was dismantled and taken by sea back to Lockheed Aircraft Service-International, at New York International Airport, then called Idlewild. Here, in what was later described as 'the most extensive rehabilitation project undertaken by a commercial aircraft maintenance and service organization in the US', it was rebuilt as N74192 before being zero-timed and sold to El Al as 4X-AKD in the spring of 1952 just 29 weeks after the wreck was unloaded at a New York City dock. It eventually came back to the UK where it was scrapped at Luton in May 1965.

Built by The Aeronautical Corporation of Great Britain Ltd at Peterborough and sold by Aircraft Exchange & Mart Ltd at Hanworth in August 1938, Aeronca 100 G-AEVT ended up during the war with the Clitheroe & District Air Training Corps. An advertisement for an aircraft engine for £17.10/- attracted the attention of Paul Simpson of Pinner who promptly responded. 'For an extra £17.10/-,' said the vendor, 'you can have the aeroplane to which it's attached!'. And so began the lengthy restoration of this aircraft which was finally completed using the wings from the Aeronca 300 G-AEVE. Restoration took from 1947 to 1950. On July 11th 1950, Simpson took off from Loughborough College Aerodrome in Leicestershire to fly to Hatch End Aerodrome near Pinner, Middlesex. An undetected line-squall struck the little

aircraft almost as soon as it was airborne, the machine stalled and crashed vertically into a narrow ditch in a field the other side of the Derby Road. Miraculously, the shallow ditch had a deep sump at the very spot into which the nose of the aircraft fell, the whole shock of impact being absorbed on bracing wires and wings. Simpson sustained two broken ankles and concussion and was pulled from the wreck by a passing lorry-driver. Very little of the wreck proved salvageable so extensive was the impact damage.

Paul Simpson's accident in Aeronca G-AEVT kept him in hospital for a long while during which time he and I managed to find another Aeronca to restore. This one, G-AEFT, had been found at Cowes on the Isle of Wight and brought across on the car ferry to Portsmouth by a young ex-RAF pilot now turned farmer who lived in Worplesdon, Surrey. His plans to restore it were thwarted by an excess of enthusiasm over skill plus the fact that the machine had lost all its bracing wires and numerous other quite important parts. We did eventually rebuild and fly G-AEFT but very little of G-AEVT went into it other than the cabane strut and the landing wires. All other bracing wires had been strained. Nicknamed after the renowned Musselburgh company that made these special streamlined-section wires, pre-flight checks on the Aeronca always entailed 'feeling the Bruntons' – a term appreciated only by those who had the skill and dexterity to negotiate their way through these button-snagging cables to enter the cabin.

Here's one I prepared earlier… Pre-war-built Luton LA.4 Minor, G-AFIR, had crashed in 1939 through failure of its 25 hp Anzani twin inverted 'V' engine. Immediately after the war I set about rebuilding it. At that time the authorities had effectively banned homebuilt aircraft in Britain and would only allow pre-war aircraft to fly again if they had a full C of A. My aircraft had previously flown on a Permit to Fly and now these had been legislated away. I had virtually rebuilt the entire aircraft with the original registration – and a new engine, an Aeronca-JAP J.99 of 37 hp. After a long battle and changing ministerial minds, I eventually flew the aircraft. I was in the Royal Air Force at the time and could only get home to fly occasionally. My local aerodrome (Elstree) had run very low on petrol and a number of aircraft had been refuelled on the dregs. Mine was one of them, after which I had put

the machine in the hangar and gone back to my Station. During my absences, some other aircraft had experienced engine trouble which had been attributed to scum from the bottom of the aerodrome tank. I came home three weeks later and, unaware of what had happened, got the aircraft out, started up and took off. I got as far as Bushey in Hertfordshire before the engine simply stopped! Unable to make my own landing strip at Hatch End and forced to a downwind landing close to the railway line at Oxhey Lane – and succeeded in hitting one of just a few trees that dotted an otherwise clear 30 acre field! It was the afternoon of May 1st 1951. The accident investigators found my fuel filter solid with Elstree's tank gunge and that's the first time I learned of the cause of the problem. Subsequently, after a new fuselage, new wings, new tail, new undercarriage and new lift-struts and new propeller, G-AFIR was back in the air. Picture by the *Watford Observer*.

An untimely conclusion to four years of hard work and the herald of another four years of ditto to make good the mess! This was the aftermath of my May 1st 1951 mishap with my Luton LA.4 Minor at Carpender's Park. The insurance assessor (briefcase visible right of nose) estimated that the damage was under the statutory 80% which would initiate payment on my policy, so they paid nothing! The rebuild necessitated a new fuselage, new tail, a pair of new wings, new lift-struts and wing pylons, new engine mounting and new propeller, new instruments and new wheels plus new cockpit seat and new harness. The registration letters were quite undamaged and were re-used. A popular comedy radio show of the time broadcast an apt sketch entitled 'Insurance: the White Man's Burden!' at which I displayed a concurring nod.

Vandalism comes in all shapes and forms and this is a story of vandalism but only after the main event. Parnall Hendy Heck 2C G-AEGI was one of those delightful forerunners of racing monoplanes made by Edgar Percival. Percival never liked it to be thought that the Gull was not his sole design but nevertheless the wing was to the patented design of Basil Balfour Henderson to the specification called for by Whitney Straight. The prototype was built for Henderson by Westland at Yeovil. It took its unusual name from the familiar name of the designer ('Hendy' Henderson) and his habit of cursing ('Oh! Heck!'). Other examples were built by Parnall Aircraft, among them G-AEGI powered by a 200 hp Gipsy Six. It was fast and became a popular racing machine, having a cruise of 160 mph, flat out at 185 mph and yet a stalling speed, with Fowler flaps, of just 40 mph. On June 17th 1950 the sole surviving Heck was entered for the King's Cup Race at Wolverhampton. It finished seventh at an average of 159 mph and was parked when Spitfire F.Mk.VB G-AISU piloted by Capt A W Wheeler careered into its tail on a misjudged landing. As seen in this picture taken moments later, damage was not extensive and in these enlightened times would be thought of as a month or two in the workshop. As it was the remains were stored for a few years and then turfed out and burned! That was the vandalism.

Right up until 1952 one could go for a joy-ride at Heathrow Airport. Island Air Services operated several DH.89a Dragon Rapides and charged 11/- for a short flight around London. The aircraft took off and landed between larger commercial traffic. On the late afternoon of August 1st 1952, G-ALBB (one-time NR741) piloted by 47-year-old Brian McGinn and with eight passengers on board, came in to land just a bit too soon after a Boeing Stratocruiser had taken off. The dangers of wake turbulence were little understood in those days. The Rapide was tossed about like a toy before being thrown to the ground on the airfield perimeter. Despite the state of the wreck, the pilot was the only one who sustained serious injury and all his passengers suffered minor damages which were remedied at the West Middlesex Hospital. This accident was thus a watershed in aviation for it led to experiments to establish just how lethal wake turbulence really was. It also put an end to joy-riding amidst the airliners at Heathrow.

The Miles Marathon was Miles Aircraft's last great civil aircraft design. The four-engined transport was still in early development when, for quite unnecessary reasons, the Miles company at Reading was declared bankrupt and work was stopped. Handley Page Aircraft Ltd, then of Cricklewood and Radlett, took over the design rights calling it the HPR 1 Marathon and put it into production. The 24th production machine was XA271 (G-AMGT) but during a test flight on September 30th 1954 a wing-tip fell off and the machine crashed at Calne, Wiltshire. Regrettably all five on board were killed. This picture shows the crashed aircraft which appears to have struck a military-registered car, seen upside down in the foreground, in its descent.

In the 1930s, aside from the de Havilland types and, predominantly, the DH.82 and DH.82A Tiger Moth, the most popular light trainer was the Avro Cadet. A scaled-down version of the equally popular Avro Tutor, it was the chosen mount for Air Service Training Ltd at Hamble for whom many were built, and also the Royal Australian Air Force. There were numerous varieties, and the nominal two-seater was built with three in a wider fuselage, some with cabins, some with wing stagger and others without. In fact, the Cadet was a whole family. The majority were powered by the Armstrong Siddeley Genet series of radial engines. However, a small number had the Gipsy Major I inverted in line with which the aircraft, having less frontal area, had an improved performance. At the end of the war, this whole dynasty of machines had dwindled to one solitary example. This was an Avro 638 Club Cadet, G-ACHP. With unstaggered wings and the Gipsy engine this had spent the war years as a communications hack by Saunders Roe Ltd at Cowes. Disposed of as surplus to post-war needs it was acquired by the Vintage Aeroplane Club at Denham and lovingly restored. It joined a tiny but choice fleet of VAC aircraft which included the Avian, G-ABEE. One of Handley Page Aircraft Ltd's flight test observers was Jock Ogilvy who lived in Pinner Hill Road, Pinner. He was engaged in early trials on the Victor 'V'-bomber and was to have a remarkable escape from death when the tail fell off on one trial: he had been asked to switch duties with another FTO. However, Jock decided to greet the New Year with a bit of flying in G-ACHP on January 1st 1956. Incredibly he took off from Denham into an approaching line-squall and the poor Cadet was literally thrown into the trees close to the airfield. Jock was unhurt but the Club Cadet's last example was no more as my photograph taken in the mist that afternoon reveals. I was not the only one to have lost a cherished friend that day.

The Luton Minor G-AHMO was built to the original 1938 LA.4 design as published in *Practical Mechanics* magazine by R S Finch of Darwin, Lancashire, but he never flew it. The aircraft was finished off by T G Thomas at RAF Cottesmore in 1966 who fitted it with one of the Popular Flying Association's stock of Aeronca-JAP J.99 engines built for The Aeronautical Corporation of Great Britain Ltd by the London motorcycle engine-makers J A Prestwich Ltd. Unfortunately the machine came to grief on my then home aerodrome – Sandown, Isle of Wight – on October 22nd 1966. Cause? A combination of bad weather, a heavy pilot and a downwind turn over high ground to the west of the airfield circuit. Some parts were used in G-ATWS.

Accidents at air shows are a mixed blessing. If serious then the public may be injured or worse as happened with John Derry and Tony Richards in the DH.110 at Farnborough's 1952 SBAC Show (28 spectators dead and 63 injured). However, the benefit (to the morbid fascination of the accident investigators) is that there's a pretty good chance that the event may be photographed, sometimes thousands of times! America's top exhibition pilot in the 20th century was Bob Hoover (born 1922) and his aerobatics in the piston-engined Shrike Commander are still talked of today. At the Hanover Air Fair in 1970 he was demonstrating a Rockwell Sabreliner N253MZ and after a stunning performance discovered that his starboard undercarriage would not lower. It was at this point that the air show organisers made their biggest blunder as, over the exhibition-wide Tannoy system came the message 'Mr Hoover has undercarriage problems and may have to crash-land!' The ensuing stampede to the airfield runway fence ensured that Hoover's low pass with partially-lowered wheels was seen by all.

Before a packed observation area, camera shutter clicking almost drowned out the engine noise as Hoover's expert one-wheeler would be photographed at least a few times! Here the wing has just struck a runway-side transformer which has exploded with a flash of flame and a little smoke but nothing else. An aileron and a flap have been removed and tossed into the sky as the aircraft, only minimally damaged ground to a halt. In an early example of what is now rampant American injustice, Hoover – a genuinely brilliant pilot – was subsequently grounded by the US authorities who spuriously believed he was medically unfit to fly.

Aircraft do not have to have an engine in order to suffer the humiliation of a crash. Some of the worst mishaps have occurred with gliders and sailplanes. Popular with Air Training Corps and Air Cadet squadrons was the side-by-side two-seat Slingsby T.21B known in the RAF as the Sedburgh. This example, WB921, was on a training flight when it ran out of 'green ball' (lift) and in attempting to stretch its glide, stalled and spun in with the result seen here. Both occupants miraculously escaped though badly injured.

A little bit like the genuine 500-year-old broom that has had fourteen new handles and a dozen new heads but is still in original condition, 1933-registered G-ACDC's claim to be the oldest surviving flying condition Tiger Moth is a bit tongue-in-cheek. To my certain knowledge it has been severely damaged on at least three occasions that I know about. Here at the Popular Flying Association Rally at Rochester in September 1963 the weather was so bad that most of the flying display had to be cancelled. Only two aircraft flew that dreadful Sunday morning – my newly-built Luton LA.4 Minor G-ASAA and veteran flyer Neville Browning in the Tiger. Clag-base was no more than 200 feet. Neville decided to attempt some low-level aerobatics to entertain a fractious crowd. Unfortunately in recovering from a slow roll he struck the ground and rolled 'ACDC into a ball in front of a now-appreciative crowd. As people rushed to help, fuel dripping from the tank vent was ignited by the hot engine and a small fire broke out right under the petrol tank. With presence of mind somebody had grabbed a handheld fire extinguisher. The flames were out in a second and Neville Browning emerged from the wreck unhurt but cursing! Norman Jones, owner of Rollasons, always said that so long as an aircraft hadn't killed somebody, he would rebuild it and so shortly afterwards, G-ACDC was flying again after a total of what must be in excess of 350% fresh parts since new!

Another view of Neville Browning's spectacular and rather public demolition of G-ACDC at Rochester.

Flying mishaps can happen to every type of man-made machine that foolishly ventures off the trusty and proven surface of the earth. Here is a picture of XP355, a Westland WS-55 Whirlwind HAR 10 attached to the Central Flying School of the Royal Air Force at South Cerney. This mishap seems to have come about through a rather heavy landing.

Another view of XP355 showing the spread mainwheels and the collapsed nosewheel and the aft fuselage tail boom break. It is likely to have been the result of a practice engine failure autorotation routine that didn't quite go according to plan.

It is not often that an aircraft accident at an airport causes so much collateral damage that the total insurance claim is many times the value of the aircraft but that was the case with Airspeed Ambassador Mk.2 G-AMAD. The aircraft had flown with British European Airways as Elizabethan class *Sir Francis Drake* from November 1952 until June of 1960 when it was sold to BKS Air Transport Ltd of Southend. Less than a month later, on the 3rd of July, it was involved in a uniquely spectacular smash at Heathrow Airport. The aircraft had been modified with a large rear freight door to enable it to undertake charter work transporting horses. On the fateful day the aircraft was carrying eight thoroughbred racehorses and a crew of three plus five grooms as it approached London's busy airport for landing. Suddenly the port flap actuating rod suffered a fatigue failure causing the instantaneous retraction of the landing flaps on that side. With one wing stalled and the other in high lift condition, the aircraft began a steep uncontrollable turn towards the central terminal area with one wing tip firmly on the ground. Had there been more space it might have been recoverable (by retracting the flaps completely) but the immediate presence of parked aircraft made that action impossible. In a sweep the Ambassador ripped the fin off Trident G-ARPI and sliced the complete rear fuselage off G-ARPT standing next to it. It now slid upside down into the side of the newly-completed Terminal 1 building and exploded. Captain Ernest Hand (who had 7,000 hours on the type) and his crew were killed along with three of the grooms and all of the horses. Miraculously only three people on the ground were injured. Trident G-ARPI was a write-off and in my picture, taken about an hour after the incident, petrol bowsers can be seen siphoning fuel from the fully-loaded wing tanks while crew members stand around in shock and disbelief. Trident G-ARPI was repaired only to crash at Staines on June 18th 1972.

In so many instances, after a jet bomber hits the ground there's not a lot left to photograph that's in any way recognisable. Just to prove that some accidents can be more embarrassing than expensive, here's what happened to Avro Vulcan XA913 at Waddington on October 16th 1962. The pilot, practising short power-on landings, managed to bang the extreme tail-cone onto the deck before the wheels. The jet pipes escaped by inches and the aircraft was repaired. Not sure what happened to the erstwhile flyer but the chances are he's paid for the damage by now. That, of course, is why naval captains always go down with their ship.

I have already spoken about airliners *plunging* to the ground. Most times these are grim events spoken of in hushed tones but what happened to Hawker Siddeley HS.748 Srs.1 G-ARMV at Lympne was very different. Terms such as 'wrapped up in a ball' generally relate to nasty prangs in small biplanes, but this unfortunate aircraft managed to roll itself up quite spectacularly all by itself – and happily nobody was seriously injured. A V Roe's 1957-designed Dakota replacement was an outstanding success right from the start and when Roe became integrated as part of Hawker Siddeley in 1964, production and development of the design proceeded apace. G-ARMV was the prototype Series 1 machine for Skyways Coach Air Ltd and made its first flight at Woodford on the last day of August 1961 before starring in that year's SBAC show. It then entered service on the Lympne-Beauvais shuttle service with Skyways on April 1st 1962. On the evening of July 11th 1965, Lympne's soft all-grass surface responded to a heavy landing by firmly grabbing the nosewheel and flipping the aircraft over onto its back. It careered 400 yards across the airfield ripping off the starboard wing and engine. Amazingly neither crew nor passengers suffered any serious injuries. This mishap highlighted the drawbacks of operating modern aircraft on unprepared grass especially after a rainy summer – shades of Portsmouth Airport's twin HS.748 accidents: plans for a concrete runway were immediately put in hand. In this view, a number of ropes have been attached to the port wing stub during attempts to pull the remains into a better position for scrapping.

Named *Deidre*, Interconnair's Bristol B.175 Britannia EI-BBY was registered on June 18th 1976 having been in military service as XL658 *Adhara*. On September 30th 1977 it crashed while landing at Shannon and caught fire. Miraculously all on board escaped serious injury and the airport hose-wizards put the fire out to leave a rather blackened but still recognisable hulk.

Dangling from a wire is the stuff of circuses, not private pilots, yet across the years it's amazing just how many fliers have been left helpless in the air, too high to jump out yet too low to do anything about it. This must be what the Americans mean when they talk of being 'hooked up'! It did, however, happen in Germany. On Sunday, August 17th 2008, 65-year-old Reinhardt Leveringhaus and his 63 year-old wife took off in their Europa light aircraft D-ELPR for a bit of pleasure flying from Kempten Durach airfield near Ulm. Approaching to land in strong low sunlight, the aircraft's propeller clipped the very top of a high-tension pylon while the starboard wheel snagged a 380,000-volt power cable, and slid along it stopping the aircraft in its tracks. For three hours they hung there in radio contact with their rescuers while being soaked in leaking petrol. Use of a helicopter was ruled out on the grounds that its downwash would throw the aircraft to the ground. Finally a huge crane was trucked in and strops positioned on the undercarriage legs were attached to a sling around the rest of the power cables to secure the machine by spreading the load. Meanwhile a 'cherry-picker' arrived and rescuers went up and opened the cockpit door. Here you can make out the passenger's right arm with hand on the coaming prior to being evacuated. Their ordeal had lasted three hours but, apart from shock, no serious injury was sustained by anybody and the aeroplane was rescued but not without sustaining what was described as 'substantial damage'.

The days of passenger-carrying airliners landing in small fields to dodge bad weather or fix defective engines are long gone. Even so, it was appreciated from earliest times that touching down in the water, unless you were a flying boat or seaplane, was even more hazardous: Handley Page W.10 G-EBMT *City of Ottawa* tried it on June 17th 1929 and four of the eleven passengers drowned as the aircraft sank. Successful unplanned water landing has been accepted as statistically impossible since that time. Small aircraft hitting water have a low survival rate. Larger aircraft are not even in the equation since break-up invariably follows contact with what the Royal Naval flyers so aptly called 'the 'oggin'. Success rates for a modern jet-airliner making a water landing are thus in the hen's teeth category of probability. All that changed when, on January 15th, 2009, a US Airways' Airbus A320-214, N106US, made a perfect touchdown in New York's Hudson River. Flight 1549 left La Guardia for Charlotte, North Carolina at 15.03 hrs local time with 146 passengers and five crew. Immediately after take-off when climbing through 3,200 feet altitude, the aircraft flew through a large flock of Canada geese putting both engines out of action. Too low for a turn-around and unable to stretch a fully-fuelled glide twelve miles to Tetaboro across the skyscrapers of Manhattan Island, 57-year-old pilot Chesley Sullenberger made for the Hudson River touching down with the current. The aircraft did not bounce but slid safely to a standstill. Bitter winter cold had brought ice to the river yet miraculously no 'heavy-ice' contact was made. All on board evacuated onto the wings from where a flotilla of pleasure boats reached them within five minutes and saved everybody. *Picture with grateful acknowledgement to Reuters' Gary Hershorn.*

See next page: The flight had lasted less than five minutes and the powerless Airbus demonstrated its robustness by retaining its integrity as it touched the water at an airspeed of approximately 115 knots. The tide was flowing very fast at about twelve knots which helped reduce the contact speed. Even so, the port engine was torn off in the touchdown, the engine pod being provided with a weak link intended to break and drop the engine free in an emergency: it was later recovered by divers. The aircraft was carried downstream very rapidly and the deployment of the rescue boats exhibited the highest quality of seamanship equal to that of pilot Sullenberger's skill in effecting the landing. Once empty the aircraft was towed to a deep-water mooring where she eventually sank. Heavy-lift cranes were brought in and, on the evening of January 17th the delicate job of lifting was begun. The task was made all the more tricky because the fuel tanks were still intact and full and it was imperative not to rupture the structure and let the volume of river water drain. In this picture the aircraft has just broken surface next to the dock wall, the starboard wing still encased in mud from the river bed. Floating slabs of ice indicate how lucky the original splask-down was. *Picture from live TV coverage recorded at the time, courtesy Steve Ryder.*

Almost an hour after breaking the surface, Captain Chesley Sullenberger's airliner emerges into clear air above the ice-covered Hudson River. Its one remaining engine shorn of pod fairings, its cargo and cabin access doors wide open along with the overwing escape hatches through which everybody was so successfully evacuated, Airbus N106US streams rivulets of water as it is gently hoisted onto a heavy duty barge prior to being towed to a dockside standing. With this final picture of my collection it is pleasing to end on a happy note with this story of the *plunging* airliner that really did 'plunge' but got away with it! *Picture from live TV coverage recorded at the time, courtesy Steve Ryder.*